The Philosophical Roots of Anti-Capitalism

Studies in Marxism and Humanism
Kevin B. Anderson, University of California, Santa Barbara and Peter Hudis, Oakton Community College

In the spirit of the dialectical humanist perspective developed by Raya Dunayevskaya (1910–1987), rooted in the thought of Marx and Hegel, this series publishes across a broad spectrum focusing on figures and ideas that are fundamental to the development of Marxist Humanism. This will include historical works, works by Dunayevskaya herself, and new work that investigates or is based upon Marxist Humanist thought.

Titles in the Series

The Dunayevskaya-Marcuse-Fromm Correspondence, 1954-1978: Dialogues on Hegel, Marx, and Critical Theory, edited by Kevin B. Anderson and Russell Rockwell
The Philosophical Roots of Anti-Capitalism: Essays on History, Culture, and Dialectical Thought, by David Black

The Philosophical Roots of Anti-Capitalism

Essays on History, Culture, and Dialectical Thought

David Black

LEXINGTON BOOKS
Lanham • Boulder • New York • Toronto • Plymouth, UK

Published by Lexington Books
A wholly owned subsidiary of Rowman & Littlefield
4501 Forbes Boulevard, Suite 200, Lanham, Maryland 20706
www.rowman.com

10 Thornbury Road, Plymouth PL6 7PP, United Kingdom

British Library Cataloguing in Publication Information Available

Library of Congress Cataloging-in-Publication Data

Black, David, 1950-
The philosophical roots of anti-capitalism : essays on history, culture, and dialectical thought / David Black.
pages cm. — (Studies in Marxism and humanism ; 2)
Includes bibliographical references and index.
ISBN 978-0-7391-7395-4 (cloth : alk. paper)— ISBN 978-0-7391-7396-1 (electronic)
1. Marxian economics—Philosophy--History. 2. Capitalism--Philosophy--History. 3. Philosophy, Marxist—History. Title.
HB97.5.B532 2013
335.4'12—dc23
2013026863

∞™ The paper used in this publication meets the minimum requirements of American National Standard for Information Sciences Permanence of Paper for Printed Library Materials, ANSI/NISO Z39.48-1992.

Printed in the United States of America

Contents

Acknowledgments

For input, advice, and discussion, I thank Kevin B. Anderson and Peter Hudis.

Responsibility for the text is all mine.

Introduction

The essays in this collection are concerned with the relation of philosophical issues to historical and cultural events, from Greek Antiquity to the globalized capitalism of the twenty-first century. Since I am a writer of mostly historical works, and not a professional philosopher, I would like to offer a brief explanation about how these essays came to be written. In the mid-1970s I was a student at Middlesex Polytechnic in Enfield, North London: an institution renowned at the time for the radicalism of its students and lecturers, and the frequency of its strikes and occupations. Having enrolled in a course on "Trade Union Studies," I took the opportunity to study the British Labor Movement in the period running up to the General Strike of 1926. Like many "post-68" political activists I imagined that there were lessons to be learned for our own time in studying the syndicalist strikes in the years preceding the First World War; the revolt of "Red Clydeside" (1918–1919); the struggles of the miners; the conflict between the Fabians and the revolutionary socialists who supported the Russian Revolution; etc. After all, fifty years on from the 1926 General Strike, the British economy was still largely industrial; union membership was twelve million strong and rising; and the economic crisis, that had begun to undermine the "Post-War Consensus," led to demands from both Left and Right for radical change.

For the activists of "New Left" in the 1970s the Soviet Union was no longer seen as any sort of model for radical change, in the way it had been for previous generations. But because Stalinism and so-called "actually-existing-socialism" still cast a shadow over radical politics, there was much discussion about what had gone wrong in Russia. Having moved on to a Humanities degree course at Middlesex, I studied the history of the Russian Revolution, and was directed by my history lecturer Norman Levy to read Raya Dunayevskaya's *Marxism and Freedom: from 1776 until Today* (1958). Dunayevskaya, having translated Lenin's *Hegel Notebooks* of 1914–1915, gleaned from them the philosophical insight that German social democracy's capitulation to German militarism in 1914 had been a dialectical transformation into its opposite from within. Also, using the dialectical categories of Marx's *Capital* to analyze the Soviet economy under Stalin's tyranny, she provided a compelling analysis of how the capitalist value-form operated through the rule of state-capitalism calling itself communism. Articulating Marx's humanism as a development of Hegel's revolution of the mind, she rejected not only "vulgar materialism," but also its organizational "practice": the vanguard party-to-lead, which the New Left, for the most part, had failed to get beyond. As an added bonus, the British edition of Dunayevskaya's book (Pluto Press, 1973) came with a preface by Harry McShane (1891–1988), a veteran Scottish Marxist whose exploits of sixty years prior I had happened to come across in Nan Milton's biography of John Maclean, known in his time (1879–1923) as the "Scottish Lenin."[1]

Before long I was in correspondence with Dunayevskaya and her organization, the News and Letters Committees, in Detroit, and was able to meet her celebrated Scottish co-thinker when he visited London. McShane, though well into his eighties by the time I met him, was physically and mentally the fittest octogenarian I have ever known—it was no great surprise that he lived to be nearly 97. Born in Glasgow in 1891, McShane became an active socialist and syndicalist in the engineers' union in 1908 and participated in the mass strikes of 1911. McShane became a lieutenant of John Maclean, and he was in contact with James Connolly, the socialist martyr of the Irish Rising in 1916. During the First World War, when Maclean was imprisoned for anti-war activities, McShane resisted conscription by deserting and going "underground." The famous "Revolt on the Clyde," in which Maclean and McShane played leading roles, culminated in 1919 with the "Battle of St. George's Square"—in which thousands of workers clashed with police—and the arrival in Glasgow of 12,000 troops sent by Prime Minister Lloyd George. In 1922, McShane joined the new Communist Party of Great Britain. In the 1930s, he traveled to Russia for "cadre training," and organized unemployed workers' campaigns in Scotland. In the 1940s, he became Scottish editor of the *Daily Worker*. In the post-war period McShane became disillusioned with the unprincipled practices of the party and its leaders' mindless subservience to Russian Stalinism. He left the party in the early 1950s and, although by this time into his sixties, returned to work in the shipyards.[2] In the late-1950s, when he retired from shipbuilding, he read *Marxism and Freedom,* contacted Dunayevskaya, and arranged meetings for her in Scotland when she visited Britain. He found her Marxist-Humanism "healthier and more acceptable than the poisonous concoction fed to trustful men and women all over the world by an intolerable army of 'Leaders' who specialise in concealing all that is human, and therefore vital, in Marxist theory."[3]

Following the Hungarian Revolution of 1956, many of the defectors from the British Communist Party drifted into Trotskyism or other forms of vanguardism. McShane did not however see Trotskyism as representing a truly radical break with the practice and ideology of the CP. One reason for this was his memory of "other ways" of thinking and organizing:

> We suffered a long time from the fact that we found it difficult to shake off the "Communist" way of seeing things. Had it not been for the fact that I had been 13 years in the movement before I joined the CP in 1922, I might never have made it. I certainly would not have made it had it not been for *Marxism and Freedom*.[4]

McShane, in positively referring back to the pre-Bolshevik British Left of John Maclean, James Connolly and Tom Bell, did not argue that the movement could be rebuilt using older forms of organization, such as syndicalism or council communism. Recalling the socialist education movement of the pre-First World War period he wrote of its shortcomings:

> It is well to recall the fact that, for many years, Marxist economics featured strongly as part of the curriculum in classes of the Labour movement. John Maclean [in Glasgow] was said to have the largest class in Europe on Marxist economics—when he was not in prison for his political activities. We are no longer justified in regarding Marx as just a brilliant economist. The philosophy that runs through Capital was deep-rooted in Marx and actuated him through his life.[5]

Harry died in 1988, just before the collapse of Communism, which he would certainly not have mourned had he lived to see it. Indeed, it seemed almost that his robust longevity was his revenge on the Communist Party, to which he had given thirty precious years of his life. Having lived to tell the tale of the twentieth-century Left in all its glory and infamy, he wanted new generations to learn the lessons. As he reflected, "I floundered about until I was in touch with Raya and *Marxism and Freedom*. The only thing that worries me about dying is the fear that I will not have made up for lost time."[6]

Despite Harry McShane's writings and activism, his semi-legendary status as the "Last of the Red Clydesiders," and the well-intentioned efforts of a small number of British proselytizers, Dunayevskaya's Marxist-Humanism had made negligible impact on the British Left by the time she died in 1987, aged 77. As regards academia this was not really surprising, considering the deadening impact the anti-humanist thought of Althusser and French structuralism had on an entire generation of Left-wing intellectuals. Nor, looking back, was it surprising that in the period of intense activism ending with the defeat of the Great Miners Strike of 1984–1985, theory (and especially philosophy) was seen as a "distraction" from the "struggle," or as needing to be kept separate, in the realm of "experts." Over two decades later however, Dunayevskaya's works are evidently much better known, and known worldwide. This is partly due to the efforts of her former colleagues and other sympathizers in keeping her works in print, with many new translations; and partly because of the widened transmission and discussion of her writings on the Internet. But also, in my view, there is more interest in her ideas because of the turn history has taken. If Marx's *Capital* has gained credibility because of the 2008 crash, so also, for some, has Dunayevskaya's defense of Marx's value-theory in *Capital* as internally consistent, indebted to the Hegelian dialectic, and totally relevant to the crisis facing humanity in the twenty-first century.

In the political sphere Dunayevskaya's disdain for any purely organizational or theoretical "solutions" to the impasse of the Left seems to have been justified by events. Before the fall of the Berlin Wall, the anti-Stalinist Left had not expected that the demise of the "Soviet" system would parallel the demise of the Socialist Idea in the West as a teleological presence, not only in social democracy, but also in the new social movements which had sprung up since the 1960s. This was not just a problem of the vanguardism and sectarianism of Trotskyist and Stalinist parties. Anarcho-syndicalism and self-management socialism counterposed collective ownership of the means of production to private property, and "spontaneism" to vanguardism and reformism. But the Anarcho-Left tended to ignore the problem of how the capitalist value-form of social mediation has been able to survive changes in property forms and political structures—changes which have often come about as a result of mass struggles and radical activism.

Joel Kovel, in a foreword to the 2000 edition of *Marxism and Freedom*, commented that Dunayeskaya's "followers" had given her a "cult-like status" and tended towards an "overestimation of radical movements."[7] There is some truth in this claim, inasmuch as those issues have surfaced in a number of disputes and divisions within U.S. Marxist-Humanism, especially since 2008. But Dunayevskaya regarded herself as a "continuator" of Marx's Marxism. She wanted to work, not with followers, but with other continuators, committed to working out a philosophically-grounded alternative to capitalism, and fighting the battle of ideas along "untrodden" paths, beyond the comfort zone of what Hegel called "private enclaves." As I see it, working political problems out philosophically can only mean actually *doing* philosophy, not just repeating Dunayevskaya's conclusions. Doing philosophy means engaging with philosophers past and present, and relating philosophy directly to workers and others involved in struggles for a better world. Overestimation of radical movements is inevitable if the forces of revolt are automatically and uncritically seen as instantiations of pre-existing (or unproven) ideas rather than as coming from thinking, rational men and women, living the contradictions of capitalism. For Dunayevskaya in the 1980s, the retreat of the Left in the face of the Reagan-Thatcher offensive into postmodernism was addressed in Hegel's *Logic*: "Far from expressing a sequence of never-ending progression, the Hegelian dialectic lets retrogression appear as translucent as progression and indeed makes it very nearly inevitable *if* one ever tries to escape regression by mere faith."[8] Dunayevskaya saw Hegel's dialectic of the Subject in "the continuous process of becoming, the self-moving, self-active, self-transcending method of "absolute negativity'." "Translating" the Hegelian absolute as a "dimension of the human being" revealed how far humanity had travelled since Aristotle:

> Because Aristotle lived in a society based on slavery, his Absolutes ended in 'pure Form' —mind of man would meet mind of God and contemplate how wondrous things are. Because Hegel's Absolutes emerged from the French Revolution, even if you read *Geist* as God, the Absolutes have so earthy a quality, so elemental a sweep, are so totally immanent rather than transcendent, that every distinction between notional categories, every battle between Reality and Ideality, is one long trek to freedom.[9]

However much Hegel ruthlessly criticized all of the ancient and modern philosophers he wrote about (for whatever reason, he paid scant attention to the philosophers of the Middle Ages), he saw them as revolutionists of the mind in the long trek to freedom. It follows then, that to talk about Freedom as a philosophical issue, one should, like Hegel, begin with the Greeks; hence the title of the essay comprising the first part of this book: "The Philosophic Roots of Anti-Capitalism."

According to Alfred Sohn-Rethel (1899–1990), who figures largely in this piece, the objective origin of abstract thought is to be found in the social nexus of exchange relations actualized by *monetary* abstraction. Sohn-Rethel and his co-thinker, George Thomson (1903–1987), located this origin in the spread of gold and silver coinage in Greek Antiquity. They argued that the power of monetary abstraction in exchange produced, for the first time in history, the cosmology of pure abstractions (the One, the Many, Being, Becoming, etc.) that we find in the pre-Socratic philosophies of Parmenides and Heraclitus. Sohn-Rethel proceeded to argue that *all* concepts in the history of philosophy—including the categories of Kant's pure reason and the absolutes of Hegel's dialectic—have produced an "objectively deceptive," timeless, universal logic.

Since the 1930s and '40s, when Thomson and Sohn-Rethel did their formative research, a mass of new scholarship on Greek Antiquity has accumulated. Richard Seaford, a present-day classical scholar, has drawn on the new findings to argue that, although philosophy involves unconscious cosmological projection of the abstract substance of money, it does not, as Sohn-Rethel supposes, *consist* of it. The abstraction involved in both money and philosophy is also related to a number of innovations of the "Greek Miracle":

democracy, tragedy and comedy, the popular religions, relations of production, private life, etc. As Seaford sees it, the western metaphysical tradition developed under the influence, not *only* of money, but also of the social forms and practices which preceded monetized society; therefore, money can be understood as the diremption and subsumption of the ancient *communal* principle of (re)distribution. I relate this subsumption of the communal principle in the slavery-based Greek democracy to Rosa Luxemburg's great insight, in her little-known essay on Slavery, that, "At the moment the Greeks enter history, their situation is that of a disintegrated gens [or primitive communism]."[10]

Sohn-Rethel and Thomson's historical analysis, which was awkwardly worked out under the ideological constrictions of 1930s Stalinism, seems to me in some respects a step backward from the original insights of Francis Macdonald Cornford (1874–1943), a Fabian socialist who was Thomson's tutor at Cambridge. Cornford's work (now unfortunately, largely forgotten) deserves a second look, especially his insights into the origins of "abstract schemes" of conception in the practices and belief systems of pre-Homeric society, and his cogent criticisms of the materialist dogmatism in Thomson's work.

Sohn-Rethel tried to circumvent the relation between Hegel's "idealism" and Marx's "materialism" by insisting that Kantian dualism reflected the realities of capitalism more faithfully than Hegel's anti-epistemological approach, which Sohn-Rethel saw as an attempt to draw all of the social antinomies and contradictions into the "immanency" of absolute spirit. I find this judgment on Hegel to be inadequate for understanding the two key points of Marx's critique of capital that Sohn-Rethel sought to illuminate: the division between mental and manual labor, and the fetishism of commodity production. This shortcoming is related to the lack of any substantial consideration of Aristotle in Sohn-Rethel's work.

Aristotle conceived of a social hierarchy of (in top-down order) *Theoria* (Theory and Philosophy), *Praxis* (Activity or Action) and *Techne* (Production). While philosophy and praxis—which together comprise the Realm of Freedom—have no ends outside themselves, production, performed largely by slaves, has ends outside of itself. Hegel, in his philosophic conception of the modern (post-French Revolution) world, attempted to dissolve the barrier Aristotle put between freedom (as praxis) and unfreedom (as production) and make them the two sides of spirit's historical self-objectification, united in the concept of free labor. Hegel appropriated Aristotle's concept of *energeia,* as representing an actualization of a potency originally immanent in the process, for his own conception of the dialectical historical process of "finding a world presupposed before us, generating a world as our own creation, and gaining freedom from it and in it."[11]

Marx, in *Capital, Volume III,* wrote that the polis of Greek Antiquity had more in common with "primitive communism," than with capitalism and feudalism. For in both the polis and primitive communism, it was the "actual community" that presented itself as the basis of production, and it was the reproduction of this community that was production's "final purpose." Marx then, like Aristotle, conceived of a society with no end outside itself. The difference is that, whereas for Aristotle the self-sufficient community of the polis was a community of free men ruling over a class of slaves and women, for Marx, socialism/communism would be a self-sufficient entity of "human power as its own end"; that is, in the words of August Blanqui (whom he much admired), "a republic without helots."

To quote Guy Debord, "Whatever was absolute becomes historical."[12] The second part of this book consists of the essay, *Critique of the Situationist Dialectic: Art, Class Consciousness and Reification.* It begins with Surrealism, and its influence on the founders of Letterists in post-World War Two France, whose ranks included the young Guy Debord. The Situationist International, founded by Debord in 1957, was throughout its fourteen-year history (1957–1971) racked by splits and schisms, and never had more than a few dozen members at any given time. And yet its role can be seen as quite historic, given the impact of Debord's book, *Society of the Spectacle*, and the Situationists' role in "detonating" the May 1968 near-Revolution in France.

Cultural theorists and historians of the 1960s have tended to ignore the importance of Debord's reworking of Hegelian-Marxism via Georg Lukács' writings on reification and commodity fetishism. One notable exception in Debord-scholarship is Anselm Jappe's book, *Guy Debord,* which seeks to locate Debord's oeuvre within Marxist thought, rather than to recuperate Debord as a canonical figure of (post)modern "art" and "culture." According to Jappe, the Situationist-inspired graffiti slogans of Paris in 1968, *"Ne travail jamais"* and *"Abas le travail"* are, in the twenty-first century, now more realizable (even necessary) than ever. I agree with Jappe that "Debord's theory is *in essence the continuation of the work of Marx and Hegel* and that its importance inheres for the most part precisely in this fact." I take Jappe at his word when he says, "I suspect that I delved too little into Debord's debt to Karl Korsch [a Marxist philosopher who was a contemporary of Lukács],"[13] and try to assess that debt. Where I depart from Jappe is in my taking up of what he sees as now being largely irrelevant: Debord's organizational anti-theory of class struggle, as related to the "Hegelian-Marxism" which figured so large in his novel view of workers' councils, and his attempt to "redefine" the proletariat in the Spectacular age.

Debord wanted to universalize the experience of "the true passage of time," which he saw his avant-garde comrades in the Paris of the 1950s as having aspired to in a way prefigured by his favorite revolutionaries in history: Jean-François-Paul de Gondi, alias Cardinal Retz, who, in the Fronde of

1648–1653, led the aristocratic struggle in Paris against absolutism; the poetical democrats of the thirteenth century Italian city-states; and the revolutionary workers of the 1871 Paris Commune. Debord quoted Marx from the *Poverty of Philosophy* on how under the rule of capital, "time is everything, man is nothing; he is at most the carcass of time" —the complete inversion of "time as the field of human development." Debord said that because in capitalism people's possession of things masks the reality that they are possessed *by* things, the ruling class "must link its fate with the preservation of this reified history with the permanence of a new immobility *within* history." This position was contrasted with that of the modern working class which, as the material mover at the "base" of irreversible social change, was no "stranger to history" and, for the first time, demanded "to live the historical time it makes."[14]

The great revolt of May/June 1968 in France marked, for Debord, "the beginning of a new era" in the struggle against the separation of humanity from its potential freedom. Twenty-one years later, in his 1988 pamphlet, *Comments on the Society of the Spectacle*, he concluded that in the new "integrated spectacle" of universalized commodification, power had established an eternal present of pseudo-cyclical time in which historical memory was literally becoming a thing of the past. In conclusion, I consider the later Debord's "pessimism" regarding revolutionary prospects, and Jappe's attempts to renew anti-capitalist thought *sans* class. For Jappe, whose work is indebted to Moishe Postone's *Time, Labor and Social Domination*, the difference between the 1960s and the present is that the politics of class are now dead, buried and irrelevant, due to the globalized triumph of a capitalism based on alienated "dead labor" and universal commodification. Neither Jappe or Postone however, offer any concept of transformation to a post-capitalist society. Postone's reading of Marx's *Capital* does offer important new insights into commodity fetishism in modern capitalism and the woeful inadequacy of Leftist critiques. Postone's argument that the subjective agency of the Proletariat can only ever be subsumed by the meta-subject of capital, has been interpreted by Jappe and others as having laid the theoretical basis for a program to "Abolish Work" through the automation that Capital develops in its drive to accumulate. In my reading of Marx's *Capital,* the living laborers who embody "labor-power" (which in its congealed, abstract form is the life and death of value production) are the irrevocable Other of Capital, although they are not the *only* potential force of its "gravediggers" and, collectively, do not *automatically* become revolutionary subjects in their everyday encounters with the Big "S": the "automatic subject" which Postone sees as defining Capital. Avoiding such "Traditional Marxist" crutches as "objective historical laws of development" and "crisis," my critique of Postone and other Leftist thinkers is from the standpoint of a philosophically grounded anti-capitalism.

Two of the essays in the third part of this book—"Labor and Value: from the Greek Polis to Globalized State-Capitalism" and "Reification in the 21st Century—Lukács' Dialectic"—were first published in the British Marxist-Humanist journal, *The Hobgoblin.* The two final essays, "Ends of History and New Beginnings: Hegel and the 'Dialectics of Philosophy and Organization'" and "Philosophy and Revolution in the Twenty-First Century" are previously unpublished.

NOTES

1. Nan Milton, *John Maclean* (London: Pluto Press, 1973).
2. Harry McShane and Joan Smith, *Harry McShane: No Mean Fighter* (London: Pluto Press, 1978).
3. Harry McShane, Review of Raya Dunayevska's *Philosophy and Revolution*, in *The Scottish Marxist-Humanist* (1974). Reprinted in *Hobgoblin No. 5* (2003).
4. Peter Hudis, *Harry McShane and the Scottish Roots of Marxist-Humanism* (Glasgow: John Maclean Society Pamphlet, 1992), p. 30.
5. Harry McShane, preface to Raya Dunayevskaya, *Marx's Capital and Today's Global Crisis* (Detroit: News and Letters Publications, 1978).
6. Hudis, *Harry McShane,* p. 31.
7. Joel Kovel, Foreword, Raya Dunayevskaya, *Marxism and Freedom* (New York: Humanity Books, 2000), p. xix.
8. Raya Dunayevskaya, Preface (1986), *Philosophy and Revolution* (Lanham, MD: Lexington Books, 2003), pp. xiii.
9. Raya Dunayevskaya, *Philosophy and Revolution,* p. 43.
10. Rosa Luxemburg, "Slavery," *The Rosa Luxemburg Reader,* eds, Kevin B. Anderson and Peter Hudis (New York: Monthly Review Press, 2004), p. 114.
11. George Wilhelm Friedrich Hegel, *Philosophy of Mind,* (Oxford University Press: 1971), p. 386.
12. Guy Debord, *Society of the Spectacle* (Detroit: Black and Red, 1983), p. *73.*
13. Anselm Jappe, *Guy Debord* (University of California Press: 1999), p. 182.
14. Debord, *Society of the Spectacle* , p. 143.

Chapter One

The Philosophical Roots of Anti-Capitalism

1 – THE "SECRET IDENTITY" OF THE COMMODITY FORM

Alfred Sohn-Rethel (1899–1990) spent his formative years in the company of the young intellectuals who went on to found the famous Institute for Social Research (also known as the "Frankfurt School"), notably, Walter Benjamin, Max Horkheimer, Siegfried Kracauer and Theodor Adorno. According to Sohn-Rethel, "the thunder of the gun battle for the Marstall in Berlin at Christmas 1918 and the shooting of the Spartacus rising in the following winter" re-echo in the subsequent writings of these radical intellectuals; they were attempting to build "the theoretical and ideological superstructure of the revolution that never happened." For his own part, Sohn-Rethel, as a student in Heidelberg during the aftermath of the defeated revolution, "glued" himself to Marx's *Capital* "with a relentless determination not to let go." Finally,

> with an effort of concentration bordering on madness, it came upon me that *in the innermost core of commodity structure there was to be found the [Kantian] 'transcendental subject'*.... the secret identity of commodity form and thought form which I had glimpsed was so hidden within the bourgeois world that my first naïve attempt to make others see it only had the result that I was given up as a hopeless case. 'Sohn-Rethel is crazy!' was the regretful and final verdict of my tutor Alfred Weber (brother of Max), who had had a high opinion of me.[1]

Sohn-Rethel was awarded his doctorate in 1928. But because of the economic slump then ravaging the German economy, he was unable to obtain an academic post. In 1931 he found employment at the offices of the industrial employers' organization, *Mitteleuropäischer Wirtschaftstag,* in Berlin. After the Nazis came to power in 1933 he found himself in a position to feed important economic intelligence to the anti-fascist underground. This he did very effectively until 1937, when he was tipped off that the Gestapo was about to arrest him. He fled into exile and reached England.

Sohn-Rethel was able to meet up again with Adorno in Oxford and discuss a 130-page typescript he had written, entitled *The Sociological Theory of Knowledge*. In this draft Sohn-Rethel was developing his thesis that the exchange of commodity values as mediated by money was the precondition of an objective process of abstraction which was in turn the precondition of abstract conceptual thought. Initially, Adorno was enthused, telling Sohn-Rethel that his findings "had triggered the greatest mental upheaval that I have experienced in philosophy since my first encounter with [Walter] Benjamin's work—and that was in 1923! This upheaval reflects the magnitude and power of your ideas, but also the depth of an agreement that goes much further than you could have suspected." Adorno wrote to Horkheimer in New York, suggesting that their Institute might consider giving Sohn-Rethel a research project. Adorno did however, add a crucial reservation: that he detected a "monomaniacal" tendency in Sohn-Rethel, which he thought was probably due to the years he had spent in forced isolation from the intellectual milieu. Horkheimer, who saw changes in philosophical categories as primarily conditioned by the social organization of labor, was skeptical of Sohn-Rethel's idea that the categories reflected forms of exchange established long before the development of capitalism. In response to Adorno, Horkheimer said that Sohn-Rethel, despite his "great intelligence," seemed to be an "idealist" offering an "eternal system." Horkheimer wrote to Sohn-Rethel, telling him that if the connections he was making between ideological and economic structures were more than just analogies then they needed to be worked out "conclusively." Relations between Sohn-Rethel and the Institute for Social Research stalled at that point and went no further.[2]

By 1951, Sohn-Rethel had worked up his *Sociological Theory of Knowledge* into a book manuscript, now entitled *Intellectual and Manual Labour: A Critique of Epistemology*. He submitted it to the publishing house of the British Communist Party, Lawrence and Wishart, only to have it rejected as being "too unorthodox." Other publishers rejected it as being "too Marxist."[3] It was finally published twenty years later, when "New Left" students of the Frankfurt School recognized Sohn-Rethel's historical importance and originality. In the 1970s, German and English publishers put out an updated version of *Intellectual and Manual Labour*, as well as his other important book, *The Economy and Class Structure of German Fascism*, which was based on his first-hand knowledge of working in the belly of the Nazi beast.

In *Intellectual and Manual Labour,* Sohn-Rethel comments on Marx's speculation in the *Critique of the Gotha Program* about the vanishing of the antithesis between mental and physical labor in the higher phase of a future socialist/communist society: "But before understanding how this antithesis can be removed it is necessary to understand why it arose in the first place." Sohn-Rethel argues that, in order to derive consciousness historically from social being, we must presuppose "a process of abstraction which is part of this being."[4] In commodity exchange, the abstractness of the action of exchange cannot be known by the participants when it happens. Because they are occupied with the use of the commodities they see in their imagination, the universal nature of the action and its implications is repressed.[5] In the exchange abstraction, "What the commodity owners do in an exchange relation is practical solipsism—irrespective of what they think and or say about it."[6] In the "exchange" between humans and nature, as takes place in agricultural societies, time is perceived as inseparable from natural events such as the ripening of the crops, the breeding of livestock, the change in the seasons, the human life-span, etc. But the "social synthesis" of commodity exchange enforces abstraction from all of this and produces an "extraordinary paradox," in which exchangeable objects in varying states of perishability are assumed to remain immutable for the duration of the transaction:

> in the market-place and in shop windows, things stand still... A commodity marked out at a definite price, for instance, is looked upon as being frozen to absolute immutability... time is emptied of the material realities that form its contents in the sphere of use.[7]

Similarly, with the endless expansion of the market, the experience of space is transformed in the distance the commodities have to travel when being exchanged. The time-space aspect is one side of a "double abstraction." The other side is the "second nature" effect of the exchange–equation in imposing on concrete labor a "reifying process," in which quantity is abstracted over quality in a manner that constitutes the foundation of free mathematical reasoning. This being the case, claims Sohn-Rethel, we would expect to find mathematical reasoning emerging at "the historical stage at which commodity exchange becomes the agent of social synthesis, a point in time marked by the introduction and circulation of coined money."[8] He finds it, as we shall see, in Greek Antiquity.

2 – THE CAPITALISM OF PHILOSOPHY? THE GREEK ORIGINS OF ABSTRACTION

Sohn-Rethel grounds the emergence of Western philosophy and scientific thought in an "autonomous intellect," which becomes separated from manual labor and production in the civilizations of Antiquity. These civilizations are formulated by Sohn-Rethel as "societies of appropriation" which displace communal and classless "societies of production." In a society of production, the communal order is derived directly from social labor and there is no appropriation of surplus product by any class of non-producers. The society of appropriation operates either *unilaterally,* as in Ancient Egypt and medieval feudalism, or *reciprocally,* as in capitalism. In the early phase of the reciprocal mode the appropriation is carried out by the "middle-man," who sells the commodity for more than he pays the producer for making it. When, in the post-feudal era, the laborer is separated from the means of production, labor-*power* itself becomes a commodity; and in time, nearly all the wealth produced goes through the sphere of circulation, and hardly anything is produced except as a commodity.[9]

Sohn-Rethel traces the autonomous intellect back to Ancient Egypt. Whereas in a society of commodity-production, thinking is rational while social production is irrational, in the Egyptian society of appropriation the irrational beliefs of the priestly ruling class are matched by planned rationality in production. The agricultural land of the Nile Delta is methodically irrigated by the state, which appropriates the annual collective surplus. During the seasons in which there is no farming work the farmers are conscripted into building temples and pyramids. The Pharaonic state organizes external trade, which brings in the technology of the Bronze Age for handicraft and other industries. But the technology does not penetrate the subservient farming community, which remains largely a Stone Age and communal mode of production. The state, in relation to the community of the laborers, remains an external appropriating power. In a notable feat of engineering, the priests of Egypt build a sort of primitive steam engine, used to animate statues. Steam from boiling vessels passes through underground pipes to an altar and activates the eyelids and the mouth of the god in a display of steamy anger. Such spectacles, according to Sohn-Rethel, illustrate the "make-believe division of head and hand" which precedes the reality. The *real* division between head and hand begins to develop because the elite, in collecting tributes and organizing their building program, need to measure, calculate and keep accounts; and so the arts of writing, numeration, arithmetic and geometry all develop for the purpose of appropriation. The introduction of *symbolic forms* marks the first independence of intellectual labor from manual labor.[10]

Francis Macdonald Cornford, in investigating how "abstract schemes" of conception came about historically, describes how the early Greek philosophers structured their thought like the geometry they inherited from the Egyptians. With determinations based on premises leading to intuitively certain conclusions, geometry became "the only science with a developed technique, which assured a continuous and triumphant advance in discovery."

> The spectacle of this growing body of universally valid truth in mathematics encouraged the belief that there was one complete and coherent system, in which all truth about the world could be formulated. It encouraged also the

> corresponding belief that human reason, whose work is to discover and know this truth, was not human, but divine.[11]

One of Cornford's most important students in the 1930s was George Thomson, a Communist Party intellectual who was studying the connection between commodity-exchange and pre-Socratic philosophy. Sohn-Rethel met Thomson shortly after arriving in England in 1937 and found him to be "the only other man I have known who had also recognized the interconnection of philosophy and money, although in a completely different field from my own." Sohn-Rethel and Thomson were each in their own way attempting to analyze abstract schemes of conception as constituted by historical forms of social synthesis. Thomson, in his work on Iron Age Greece, sees the social synthesis as involving the development and expansion of metal-working, agriculture, military conquest, chattel slavery and—crucially, as we shall see—coined money as currency.

Thomson, in *The First Philosophers*, says that, just as the Solonian Revolution separates society from nature as a moral order peculiar to humans, so the first Greek philosophers separate nature from society, as an external independent reality, worthy of study.[12] The Milesian philosophers project a material principle—water for Thales, air for Anaximenes—through which homogeneous substance becomes heterogeneous. In contrast to the cosmogony of Hesiod's gods, whose powers are strictly limited, the new material principles project an *unlimited* substance which maintains its identity in its transformations. But the material transformations, such as the back-and-forth from ice to water to air weaken the monist principle and suggest multiplicity rather than oneness. Anaximander attempts to overcome this contradiction by considering the highest level of unity as having an *intelligible* rather than *material* quality: a unity known through the mind rather than the senses. In Anaximander's concept of the self-manifesting unlimited (*apeiron*), the principle of everything becoming and passing away is itself the infinite, the undetermined which needs nothing outside itself. As the source of everything that is finite, limited, and changeable, the unlimited is itself unchangeable.[13]

Cornford, in *From Religion to Philosophy* (1912), says that what the Milesian philosophers meant by *physis* was the ultimate living stuff the world was made of. According to Thales, the universe is alive, has soul, and is full of daemons. In tracing the origins of this notion of ultimate, primary stuff in Nature, the first port of call for Cornford is the ancient poets. Hesiod expresses the conviction that Nature is by no means indifferent to right or wrong; when humans do what is just and right, their cities prosper, their crops flourish and children resemble their parents. In Sophocles' *Oedipus Rex*, the very earth itself is poisoned by the protagonist's unconscious incest and patricide. Cornford writes,

> When we have gone back to Homer, most scholars will think that we have touched the pillars of Hercules, and that we had better not pry into the prehistoric darkness, which the accidents of tradition have left blank. But the problem, why the Greeks believed that the Gods themselves were subject to the moral, yet impersonal and purposeless, ordinance of Destiny, is too fascinating to be abandoned, and lures us to push out into the misty ocean of hypothesis.[14]

The hypothesis is the notion—traceable back to pre-religious magic—of a primary stuff that was both natural and moral. Cornford describes how abstract schemes latent in ancient cosmogony produce the idea of a primal unity of elements which then diverge from each other as opposites, as "in meteoric phenomena and in the production of living things, plants and animals."[15] In the Milesian cosmogony the four elements of earth, air, wind and fire interpenetrate as contraries. Things perish into the elements they come out of, but these elements, as secondary substances, are themselves transient, limited and destined to return to where they came from: the ultimate "unlimited substance," which is incorruptible and undying. Because, according to Anaximander, the elements, grouped as contraries, are constantly in conflict and encroaching on each other's regions, there is a "necessity" for their being limited by a higher, "divine" power; for otherwise the war between them would result in one element destroying all of the others. As opposed to a religious treatise, Anaximander produces a work of *theory* (a cosmogony), but in trying to do away with the theological superstructure, he unwittingly recreates the magical representation which preceded it. In eliminating the gods from the cosmogony, Anaximander in effect restores *Moira* (fate, or destiny) as a collective representation of the world order. Anaximander's view of the state of nature as akin to a system of robbery and appropriation, but also as moral and just, seems paradoxical and preposterous. But if we allow that Anaximander had in his mind from the beginning some traditional representation of the order of nature familiar to his audience, but restated in rational terms, free of theological considerations, then his philosophy begins to make sense. In Hesiod and Homer we find the Olympian gods subordinated to a remote power, much older than themselves (or their Titan predecessors), that is both primary and moral. The gods—like the elements—are assigned to their provinces through the balancing of *Dike* (justice) and *Ananke* (necessity) on the scales of destiny. In the custom *(nomos)* of the tribal group this power is projected or extended to the supernatural ordering of the cosmos. The separate "departments" of nature—earth, air, wind and fire—are unified magically within the Moira system of moral boundaries imposed by custom and taboo.

In Cornford's analysis, which is influenced by the sociology of Emile Durkheim, pre-religious magical practices are the collective consciousness of the tribal group rather than forms of social control validated by a priestly individual or caste within a hierarchy. Primitive magical practices are not representational, but real facts of human existence. In Durkheim's reading of the anthropological studies of aboriginal societies, in "pure totemism" the "savages" see the human and non-human as identical. In magical rituals the rain dancer and the "Emu-Man" do not dance mimetically in the sense of conscious imitation, but in the sense of achieving emotionally what they believe in: their identity with the totem. Ritual magic is from the beginning a representation only of the collective life—or soul—of the group; the ritual is not directed towards any natural force other than the *human* group. Only with the breakdown of the collective satisfaction produced by mimetic magic does representation of the non-human arise. Once nature becomes for the group something external, self-willed and mysterious its superhuman or supra-individual power gives rise to the notion of the "divine," and the making of gods begins.[16]

In the disintegration of the Greek *gens,* tribal custom gives way to the divinities of "justice" and "necessity." In Anaximander's famous fragment:

> The non-limited is the original material of existing things, the source from which they derive their existence and to which they return at their destruction, according to necessity; for they give justice and make reparation to one another for their injustice, according to the arrangement of time.[17]

Cornford sees in this fragment the evolution of the human world through differentiation out of a primitive nucleus. This primary nucleus, as the primitive horde, divides into tribes. Under the principle of *Moira* all members of the tribe are entitled to an equal share of their products of collective labor and booty of plunder. Although the tribes co-operate with each other in production, war and intermarriage, there is no lasting peace between them.[18] Thomson agrees with Cornford that, in the fragment just quoted, "Anaximander has described the encroachment of one substance on another in terms of a feud or vendetta between rival clans." In Anaximander's idea of retribution for transgressions against non-limited power Thomson sees a reflex of the class struggle, in which the communal principle of justice through measure and limitation is reinterpreted in the interest of aristocratic power "according to necessity." In the early Greek literature on the goddesses, Thomson writes, "there arises by the side of Moira the Orphic figure of *Ananke* or Necessity. . . A century later, in Plato's *Republic*, Ananke usurps the place of Moira and is even equipped with her spindle."[19]

Parmenides, a later pre-Socratic philosopher, sees Moira, Dike, and Ananke all as "One," and he makes no Solonian distinction between nature and society. Said to have been trained in the Pythagorean mathematical method, Parmenides makes the first attempt in the history of philosophy at a pure, relentless, deductive logic of non-empirical abstractions. According to

Parmenides' logic—which is counter-intuitive in the extreme—if we rely on our senses, we might think that things are moving in their multiplicity within space and time; but, if we grasp the reality of the world as united in the *One* that is nowhere and nowhen, then we recognize the true realm of reason, in which existence simply is, and non-existence simply is not, whether in being or—what is the same thing—in thought. Everything is immovable, because movement requires empty space, and empty space is nothing and so cannot be. The thought of nothing negates the negation that nothing represents, because the thought of nothing is a something—because it is a thought. This negated nothing is made concrete in the form of limitation, for it is necessary that Being defines a limit around itself, spherical in shape, so that, though boundless, it will not be incomplete.[20]

Thomson sees this method of philosophical abstraction as an unconscious projection or reflex of the substance of exchange value.[21] Sohn-Rethel, incorporating this thesis into a general theory of the relationship between commodity-exchange and intellectual abstraction, sees Parmenides as the first exponent of "pure thought" to emerge with "a concept fitting the description of the abstract material of money." For in the Being constituted as the One we see the imperishability and universality of the standardized precious metal coinage in relation to particular, perishable commodities. Money provides the new world of exchangeable goods with a Oneness, in which an infinite variety of goods is subjected to a single standard of value in exchange, represented by a standardized piece of metal whose use value is estranged from it. In this Oneness, money can serve as "the generally recognized equivalent of all other commodities," and in its value represent "quantitative parcels of social labor in the abstract." The concept of Being as thought-producing-itself, and thought as Being-thinking-itself, resembles the idea that, in a "causal" sense, useful things make money and money makes useful things. Sohn-Rethel sees in Parmenides' projection a self-reference to the material that money "should" be made of but cannot be made of; so, as what "ought" to be, the concept prescribes itself as the correct way to reason about reality.[22] The commodity abstraction underlying the monetary service of the coins "allows for, and indeed enforces the formation of non-empirical concepts of pure thought when the abstraction becomes mentally identified in its given spatio-temporal reality." Sohn-Rethel sees the basic principles of the Greek philosophers as abstract composites of conceptual elements originating in the social synthesis of commodity exchange: "Once the elements of the real abstraction have assumed conceptual form, their character, rooted in social postulates, evolves into a dialectic of logical argument, attached to the concepts."[23]

Contra Parmenides' conception of the One as self-sufficient and immovable being, Heraclitus presents a *Logos* in which being and not-being are mediated by *becoming* in the gathering and conception of everything in its totality, through contradiction and the blending of opposite principles. Heraclitus says, "there would not be attunement without high and low notes nor any animals without female and male, both of which are opposites." But the Logos of Heraclitus has no transcendent Pythagorean principle of ultimate harmony in Elysium Fields, blessed by the goddess. Custom and tradition, as works of humans, are inconstant, for humans remain in strife with one another. Homer's wish, "that conflict might vanish from among gods and men," is dismissed by Heraclitus as "wrong," for "war is shared and conflict is justice, and all things come to pass in accordance with conflict," and war is "father of all and king of all; and some he has shown as gods, others men; some he has made slaves, others free."[24]

Sohn-Rethel pays almost no attention to Heraclitus. But according to Richard Seaford, in *Money and the Early Greek Mind – Homer, Philosophy, Tragedy* (2004), the opposition between Heraclitus and Parmenides can be seen as expression of the opposition between money as the communal logos of circulation and money as the abstract oneness of value detached from circulation.[25] Thomson, however, who reads the separation of idealism and materialism into pre-Socratic philosophy, regards Heraclitus' "dialectic" as a "materialism" which is "already pregnant with its opposite"; the "transition" from Heraclitus to Parmenides marks "the passage from quantity to quality in the evolution of idealism." For Thomson, because Heraclitus' dialectic could not itself become "idealist," it was incapable of "unconsciously" projecting monetary abstraction as conceptual thought.[26]

As Thomson and Sohn-Rethel both see the conflict between idealism and materialism in terms of class, the next section will consider the impact of the class struggles and changing social structures in Greek Antiquity on the development of philosophical abstraction.

3 – RETHINKING THE "ORIGINS OF ABSTRACTION"

"At the moment the Greeks enter history, their situation is that of a disintegrated gens." So writes Rosa Luxemburg in her essay on Slavery.[27] The gens is what Sohn-Rethel refers to as the "society of production" based on the village commune of the clan society, and what Marx refers to as "primitive communism" or the "mark." Marx's notes on primitive communism in his *Ethnological Notebooks* of 1879–1882 trace the process of dissolution in the village commune, as differentiations in rank laid the basis for the transformation into opposites, i.e., of gens into caste and aristocracy. These transformations are not viewed as successive stages, but rather, as Raya Dunayevskaya puts it, as "co-extensive within the communal form."[28] Marx highlights the internal dualisms of the egalitarian commune more than Engels does in *Origin of the Family*. Similarly, Luxemburg, who probably had little or no knowledge of Marx's unpublished ethnological notes, is explicit in criticizing Engels' view that slavery was the first great form of servitude and that slavery became a means of production only after the emergence of private property relations:

> It is necessary that one trace out the manner in which slavery emerged out of the mark and the gentile constitution. If we search for the point after which we see the mark and the gens exhibiting the oldest forms of exploitation and servitude, we will not immediately encounter slavery but other forms which might lead to slavery. Unlike Engels, we do not need to place exploitation after the emergence of private property. The mark itself allows for exploitation and servitude. The grafting of a foreign mark onto another allows for and creates a relationship of exploitation and servitude *toward the outside.*[29]

Luxemburg points out that when the Dorians conquer the collectivized people of Crete they appropriate the entire annual produce surplus to subsistence. In Sparta on the other hand, the conquest results in a different form of "collectivism": the land itself is occupied by the Dorians, and the enslaved Helots become the collective property of the new state.[30] In the mark, before monetization, trade only takes place with those outside of the mark's boundaries. Since the mark trades as one unit, the traditional clan leaders assume responsibility for commerce, which in time becomes their main activity. In their role as public officials, the clan leaders accumulate wealth; and because their positions become hereditary, they transform themselves into an aristocracy and receive tributes from the peasants in the form of produce. In Greece, with monetization, the peasants are squeezed by debt and interest. Peasants who cannot pay their debts are reduced to slavery or working for the aristocrats in building military fortifications. The new ruling class live in the fortresses, where they are joined by the free artisans, merchants, soothsayers, etc. and slaves whom they employ as personal servants—especially women concubines, wet-nurses and maids. The aristocrats develop a taste for Oriental textiles, metals and perfumes, which they obtain by trading wine, olive oil and silver.[31]

The debt slavery of the peasantry leads to revolution. The peasants, trying to turn the clock back to regain a measure of the equality enjoyed by their ancestors, demand reallocation of the land. The Solonian Revolution does not give them this, but it does, in 594 BCE, abolish debt slavery in return for the peasants accepting full obligations to fight for the state and finance its wars. Geoffrey Ste. Croix, in *Class Struggle in the Ancient Greek World,* maintains that although most of the labor in Greek Antiquity is carried out by free smallholders, tenant farmers and artisans, the surplus labor that guarantees the self-sufficiency of the polis is squeezed out of slaves. Not only do the magnificent achievements of Greek art, literature and philosophy rest on slavery, so also does Athenian democracy. Democracy does give some protection to the poorer citizens at the expense of the rich, but all of the free citizens make the most of the classes below them. The development of slavery is at its most intensive where democracy is strongest.[32]

Richard Seaford draws on the mass of modern scholarship on Greek Antiquity that has accumulated since the 1930s and '40s when Cornford and Thomson produced their most important works, and offers his own work as the first attempt to relate the most important texts of Greek Antiquity to monetization. Seaford argues that the western metaphysical tradition developed under the influence, not *only* of money, but also of the social forms and practices which preceded monetized society, however remote. Although philosophy involves unconscious cosmological projection of the abstract substance of money, it does not, as Sohn-Rethel supposes, *consist* of it.[33] Seaford argues that the Thomson/Sohn-Rethel thesis on money and abstraction, despite its originality and importance, claims too little and too much. It claims too little because the Parmenidean One does not mark a sudden break with previous thinking; rather, it is the culmination of a tendency towards single-principle abstraction already present in the earlier cosmologies of Thales and Anaximander, in whose constructions of the "unlimited" we can already see exchange-value as a factor.[34] It claims too much in its implication of a "one-to-one relation" (as reflex or projection) between Parmenides' One and the substance of exchange-value. According to Seaford, the rapid development of a new kind of money (coinage), whose *only* function was to embody exchange value, is only *one* of a series of factors making for the representation of reality as the abstract One.[35]

In investigating the origins of coined money, Seaford argues that monetization cannot be explained by the technological developments which allowed for the making of coins: metal-forging and molding had long been established in parts of the Near East, as had gold and silver bullion as means of exchange in the sea trade. According to Aristotle, the commensurability that currency brings to things is merely a convention, which originates in the process of trade. Money is able to mediate the apparent contradiction between the intrinsic differences in the goods and their abstract commensurability because the metal, useful in itself, has been made easy to handle and defined by weight—the stamp on the coin saves the trouble of measurement. As Seaford points out, the conventional validity of the coins is based on the disparity between their potential use-value (they can be melted down and transformed into useful objects) and their actual exchange-value (which exceeds the former). But this conventional validity of the coins requires and facilitates the communal confidence that the money value is permanent and will not revert to its material value.[36]

It is significant that for Aristotle the function of coinage is *koinonia*, meaning communality.[37] For in Seaford's hypothesis, what allows monetization to take hold in the Greek world before anywhere else is the synthesis of the *new* need for commensurability of goods-in-exchange with the *old* principles of communal (re)distribution. These old principles are manifested in the equal distribution of land use and produce (Moira) and the booty of plunder. But most importantly, they are also manifested in the communality of the sacrificial feast, in which all present partake equally of the distribution of roasted meat. The sacrifices of animals are enacted in religious sanctuaries, which take in donations, not only of the animal sacrificial victims, but also of durable objects associated with the sacrifice, such as metal figurines of the animals and of the deities, iron tripod cauldrons and roasting spits. In the transitory act of sacrifice these metal artifacts find permanent embodiment in the sanctuary. Some reciprocation may be expected and for the donor, whose identity remains associated with his dedication. The equality of the feast serves as a precondition for the communal confidence in symbols of identical value which makes for the adoption of coinage. The iron roasting spits, which are invested by the collective emotional contact with the deity as well as the equal distribution of the meals, are portable, useful in themselves, have value as metal, and are standardized. The standardization confers mass production and substitutability, and provides what Seaford sees as the link between the practice of sacrifice and the communal standardization of pieces of metal that is a precondition of coinage. During the pre-monetary "transition" phase, in some states the output from silver mines is distributed annually among the citizens. Later the stores of precious metals in the sanctuaries are transformed into bullion, and then coins. This facilitates the payment of the citizen soldiers in the wars against the Persians, and the payment of mercenaries employed by the tyrants. As befitting the temple, the stamp on the coin features the figure of the local deity, and soon enough, the local tyrant. The low-value silver coin of the Greeks (*obol*) takes its name from the spit (*obelos*) and the higher-value coin (*drachma*) from a handful of spits. In the communal sacrificial feast the relation of the participants to each other and their deities is reciprocal and personal; the communal principle is thus projected as a cosmic power personified in transcendent human institutions. But money, as projected *unconsciously* by the philosophers, introduces a cosmological transcendence which conceals both its interpersonal relations and its origins as an impersonal power that is also social and universal.[38]

4 – COMEDY AND TRAGEDY

Seaford sees a deep connection between monetization, Dionysian ceremony and the development of Greek theater. Although the forms of Greek drama do not appear to have been developed within the specific forms of the Dionysian ceremonies, it may well be that the riddling language of satyric drama, dithyramb and, to some extent tragedy, originates in the ritual of Dionysian initiation. In the *Dionysia* spring festival, founded by the tyrant Peisistratos in mid-sixth century BCE, dithyrambs (hymns to Dionysius) and dramas are performed at the theater in a competition (the prize is a bull, representing an incarnation of Dionysius). According to Plato, in the *Laws,* the origins of Dionysian initiation rites and the mimicking of *satyrs* in the processions of the *thiasos* lie outside of the polis in the countryside. When the *satyrikon,* as drama, does take place in the polis, the tension between the "outsider" and the polis is acted out in the conflict between the satyrs and the "straight" characters (such as Odysseus in Euripides' *Cyclops*).[39] Here comedy plays on the failure of the old world to recognize the new; and one thing that is new is commercial prostitution. In Euripides' satyr-play *Skiron,* there is talk of a prostitute exchanging favors for horses or virgins, which happen to appear as the stamped emblems on the coins. The rent boys in Aristophanes' *The Clouds* ask for payment, not in coins but in "horses" and "hunting dogs," so as to maintain the pretense of a personal relation with the buyer and the illusion of themselves as being of the "better sort." Here comedy represents, as Seaford comments, "not so much a denial of the indiscriminate impersonality of money as the failure, in the ancient Dionysiac world of the satyrs, to recognize its abstraction."[40]

In Greek tragedy, Seaford sees the transcendent power of money to efface all customary distinctions converging with the ancient unifying power of mystery cult and communal reciprocity. The struggle between unity and fragmentation can be seen in Euripides' play *The Bacchae.* The tyrant Pentheus conspires with Apollo to expose the secret of the Dionysian mystery cult. But the god Dionysius, disguised as a man, tricks Pentheus into disguising himself (as a woman) and arranges to have him discovered as an intruder and torn to pieces by the women of the cult. Of the blending and clash of opposites Seaford comments, "In Pentheus, as in the vision of Parmenides, the self-sufficiency of the man of money combines with the isolation of the mystic initiand."[41] By implication it shows that the illusion of Parmenidean self-sufficiency is undone within the Heraclitian logos where opposites are unified in the destructive movement of becoming.

Monetization marginalizes communal reciprocity and extends the tyrannical power brought about by the use of paid mercenaries. Among the nobility, money promotes an illusory individual autonomy which in reality depends on the socially constructed acceptance of the value of money and its power to circulate beyond the control of any individual.[42] In Aeschylus' *Oresteia,* Clytemnestra welcomes the returning Agamemnon at the door of his home with a blood-red tapestry made of expensive textiles. She invites him to trample on the tapestry as befitting an all-powerful ruler with no material needs, which he does reluctantly. Having tricked Agamemnon into giving way to his hubris, Clytemnestra later uses the tapestry to ensnare and murder him in revenge for his sacrifice of their daughter, Iphegenia. Seaford sees the textiles as representing the unlimited wealth of the sea trade that gives Agamemnon the illusion of unlimited power.[43]

The endogamous practices of the Greek nobility are a means of preserving wealth within the family; but in tragedy, Seaford points out, "endogamy is associated with blindness, darkness." Whereas the new society demands the circulation of money as well as females, Sophocles' Theban tyrants hoard gold and female kin below ground. In philosophy, the theme of money and incest is taken up by Aristotle, who says that interest is an "unnatural" mode of acquisition because, as production of like-by-like, it transgresses the "natural" role of currency as means for exchange and circulation of wealth. The unlimited monetized power of the tyrants is condemned by Aristotle, who says that the free man ruling over his *oikos* is only self-sufficient to the extent that he is part of the self-sufficient polis; for unity to prevail, in the face of the unlimited power of money and greed, the polis must limit itself in terms of its size, population and class inequalities.[44] Aristotle was of the opinion that acquisition of wealth within the oikos was "natural" whereas commerce had to do with "production of goods, not in the full sense but *through their exchange*" (emphasis in the original). The wealth derived from this latter form of acquisition he saw as "unnatural" and "without limit."[45] Its unlimited nature did not suit the order of the polis.

5 – THE POIESIS OF ORPHEUS – FRAGMENTATION AND WHOLENESS

According to Seaford, what is new in the Greek philosophical idea of the universe is "an intelligible order subject to the uniformity of impersonal power" and a single substance underlying the plurality of sensuous experience. It becomes metaphysical in its recognition of oppositions: reality versus appearance, original versus derivative, and total versus partial.[46] "In Heraclitus and sometimes in tragedy the transcendent power of money to unite opposites, to efface all distinctions between things and even between people, converges with the ancient power of mystery cult to unite opposites."[47]

In the Eleusinian cult, Demeter represents the womb, the grave, earth, fruit, and, most importantly, grain for agriculture, which is her great gift to humankind. When Demeter's daughter Persephone is abducted and carried off to the Underworld, Demeter becomes an "angry one" (*erinye*) and causes drought on the land, thus depriving the gods of offerings. Zeus brings about a compromise in which Pluto allows Persephone to spend some months of the year in the upper world; and so seasonal fertility of the land is established and the balance of the cosmos is restored in a new order. In the Eleusinian ritual, the initiate, under the guidance of the *hierophantes,* is made to experience, alternately, light and darkness, and hope and fear. In experiencing a divine intimacy with the Goddesses, he shares their sufferings and partakes of their sublime higher existence.[48] According to the Roman Bishop Hippolytus, the climax of the Eleusinian vision is the initiate being shown an ear of ripe corn, perhaps "magically" out of season, which represents the power of the earth mother. [49] Aristotle says of the cult of Orphism that the initiate "was not expected to learn or understand anything, but to feel a certain emotion and get into a certain state of mind, after first becoming fit to experience it."[50]

Whereas the Olympian gods are daemons of particular localities, the mystery gods, Dionysus and Orpheus, are daemons of human groups. In the state religion the Olympian gods have a political function; admission to places of worship is open to all citizens. The function of mystery cults is, in contrast, strictly religious; there are for the wandering divinities no fixed places of worship. The organization is the secret society in which admission takes place through initiation rites. For the cult of Dionysus, human existence is the cyclical life of the seasons. The conceptual framework is thus temporal, rather than spatial. The intoxicating spirit of Dionysus is human; the rituals of his *thiasmos* draw the god into the group or make the individuals lose themselves in the community of the divine and the One. As Cornford puts it,

> Orgiastic ritual ensures that Dionysus, even when his worship was contaminated with Olympian cults, never became fully an Olympian. His ritual, by perpetually renewing the bond of union with his group, prevented him from drifting away from his province, as the Olympians had done, and ascending to a remote and transcendental heaven. Moreover, a mystery religion is necessarily monotheistic or pantheistic.[51]

In Orphism, which is less "earthly," the wheel of life is governed by the circular movement of the stars. The Orphic reformation of the Dionysian religion involves a return to worshiping the heavenly bodies—especially the Sun—as measurements of Time. The other crucial difference is the personal nature of the soul; the emphasis is on salvation and returning to God in heaven, rather than becoming one with earthly nature through the ecstasy of Dionysiac ritual. Orpheus' fleeting victory in singing his way into the Underworld to win back his dead lover Eurydice is another of the cult myths which represents, according to Seaford, "the victory of unity over fragmentation in both cosmos and self." [52] The idea that where there is strife, Eros reunites, is alien to the nobility, who have gained power through division and conflict. The tyrant Peisistratos, in his campaign to break down the privileges of the old nobility, gives official encouragement to the popular cults.[53]

According to Thomson, the myth of Orpheus and Eurydice may owe its appeal as a legend of the struggle against imprisonment to the conditions in the real "underworld" which forms the economic basis of tyrannical rule.

Peisistratos pays his mercenaries with the revenues of the silver mines; and before the defeat of the Persians opens up the Orient, slaves are not yet available to work the mines. So in this period the mines are worked by peasants recently dispossessed of their land. Miners, who include women and children, may identify strongly with the characters of Orphic legend imprisoned in the underworld. Plato's parable of the cave echoes the Orphic dualisms of darkness and light, imprisonment and freedom, body and soul.[54]

The oppositions expressed in mystery cult—between limited and unlimited, individual and community, and fragmentation and wholeness—may also provide, as Seaford speculates, a "traditional model" for the oppositions in money, as projected by the philosophers. The idea of experiencing the wholeness of self in the presence of the One through mystic initiation occurs in Plato's *Symposium,* where the priestess Diotima says that beauty is revealed to the initiated as distinct from all things that partake of it and as unchanged by their passing in and out of being. This may suggest, according to Seaford, that "The mystic notion of a *concealed* fundamental truth may be adapted to—or even stipulate—the new cosmological idea (however counter-intuitive) of a concealed impersonal reality *underlying* appearances;" and that "the transcendent mystic object is unconsciously fused with the transcendence of monetary value."[55]

Plato, despite his anti-materialist outlook, approves of money because it renders things homogeneous and commensurable. The Guardians in Plato's *Republic,* despite the monkish lifestyles that Plato assigns to them, have gold and silver in their "souls," and are free from "the polluting human currency of the majority." In this way, Seaford says, "Plato's *divine* precious metal combines its traditional immortality with the socially constructed, necessarily unchanging, impersonal and invisible value of coined precious metal, located in the soul. . ." The absorption of individual things into their ideal unity consists of sublimated monetary value, which becomes the source of "being beyond being." Thought autonomously acting on thought is imagined as in a way which resembles money producing interest in likeness to itself.[56]

6 – HEGEL'S MINERVA

For Sohn-Rethel, all concepts in the history of philosophy have "one common and all-pervasive mark: the norm of timeless universal logic," and all need to be understood "historically" as "objectively deceptive." The Parmenidean One, the Platonic *nous,* the Aristotelian *actus purus*, the Kantian "pure reason" and the Hegelian Absolute are all locked in the same false consciousness of timelessness. Sohn-Rethel sees Hegel as an "unsuitable" object for his critique, because Kantian dualism is "a more faithful reflection of the realities of capitalism" than can be found in Hegel's approach, which "discarded the epistemological approach altogether" in attempting to draw all of the antinomies and contradictions into the "immanency of the mind."[57] In order to assess Sohn-Rethel's judgment on this, Hegel's thinking on the Greek philosophers needs to be considered.

Hegel, in his *Lectures on the History of Philosophy*, says that philosophically, Plato "grasped in all its truth Socrates' great principle that ultimate reality lies in consciousness, since according to him the absolute is in thought and all reality is thought." In the Platonic Idea, the identity of being and intelligibility is in itself concrete and expresses the universal as the objective, the end and the Good. [58] Plato sees the philosophical understanding of the soul as essential for those running a harmonious, organic society. He divides the *poiesis* of the soul into three parts: the rational, which desires wisdom; the passionate, which desires honor and power; and the concupiscent, which desires food, comfort, sex and procreation. The threefold division corresponds to the hierarchy of classes in the Republic. At the top of the social pyramid are the Philosophers. Below them are the Guardians, who enjoy power in education and administration, or honor in the military. At the base is the Multitude, consisting of the artisans, laborers, farmers and merchants (according to a widely held view, there is no mention of slaves in Plato's *Republic* because he presupposes slavery as the obvious economic basis for any society). The Guardians do not own property and are required to live ascetic lifestyles. Their material sustenance and housing, etc. are provided for by the productive multitude, through the state. At the top of the Republic, the ruling community of philosophers practice amongst themselves communism—owning all things in common—and allow women equal status. Plato argues that the masses can never be educated to the point of being able to have any say in government. But he also excludes from government the seekers of wealth and pleasure in the ruling class whose desires are as uneducated as those of the multitude. The only education that could benefit the excluded would consist of moral truths, taken on trust from philosophers, but presented in non-philosophic forms such as fable and myth.[59]

For Plato, truths are universal ideal forms which are as timeless as the soul. Because a long and arduous journey of the mind is needed to approach the ultimate Form of the Good, he thinks the philosophers should rule the *kallipolis*—his ideal projection—even though he knows they will never rule the existing *polis.* As Gillian Rose points out, Hegel, in his preoccupation with the contradictions of bourgeois society, sees Plato's Republic as having been misread as a utopian "dream of abstract thinking" because Plato "displayed only the substance of ethical life (absolute ethical life)" and excluded particularity and difference in the form of private property relationships. "Instead," Rose continues, "the Republic should be read as a one-sided analysis of a society which presupposes the relations which Plato sought to exclude. Hegel sought to avoid such one-sidedness, to show that ethical life is not a utopia but inseparable from relative ethical life."[60]

In philosophical terms, Hegel considers that Plato, in arguing that the particularities of the sensible world are explained through their universals, ultimately fails to show that there are any necessary internal relations between form and instance, and between reality and appearance. In Plato's dialectic the principle of negativity goes no further than "an abrogation of opposites," where one of the opposites—the universal form—is itself unity.[61] The external determination appears to be of the same order as the imaginary guardians who impose their eternal truths on Plato's ideal republic. Hegel finds Aristotle's metaphysics more convincing. Whereas Plato posits a universal that is only implicit, and effectively inert, Aristotle offers his *Metaphysics* as the science of what belongs to Being, both implicitly and explicitly. The pre-Socratics had shown that something cannot come from nothing, but Aristotle shows that being can proceed from the *partial* nonbeing of privation: "Nature is like a runner, running her course from nonbeing to being and back again."[62] In *The Physics*, Aristotle sees change as occurring according to the three principles of form, privation and material substrate. The tension between being and nonbeing characterizes the relation of the individual substance to its achievable goal or end. The deprived matter seeks form, and the form, which completes itself in actuality, aspires towards its perfect form as the realization of the Good. The highest good is the absolute truth of the divine intellect, which the human intellect is a finite instance or reflection of. In contrast to the God of the "Aristotelian" Scholastics, it would seem that for the Philosopher in the *Metaphysics* the *nous,* as the divine intellect which is always and only thinking-upon-thinking, has no knowledge of, and no concern with, anything outside itself. As the "unmoved mover" it is always and only thinking-upon-thinking, and could not possibly act on objects outside itself without undermining its self-sufficiency. It can only cause movement by being loved by the eternal substances of the first heaven, the sphere of the fixed stars which imitate it in the only way they can: in eternal, circular movements. In the sub-lunar world, love, hate and all other human emotional states are attributes of the person, not of the intellect, and thus perish along with the person. But the intellect (*nous*), according to Aristotle in *de Anima,* is something more divine and something impassive. Thought, in reception to intelligible form, actualizes its potency by becoming what it thinks when the form of the thing enters consciousness in abstraction and interacts with other forms in the making of judgments, syllogisms, etc. According to Hegel, this means that the direction of thought on objects transforms them into their truthful existence as thoughts, and constitutes their absolute substance. In considering form in the hierarchy of ends that tend towards pure actuality (the Scholastics' *actus purus*), Hegel interprets Aristotle's tripartition of substances as: 1) the sensible substances of the corruptible world; 2) the passive *nous* which becomes eternal substance in its activity; and 3) the divine thought of the unmoved mover.[63] However, as Alfredo Ferrarin points out, "eternal substance" in Aristotle's *Metaphysics* doesn't mean the incorruptible form of the intellect; it means the *stars* (the first heaven).[64] For Hegel, like many philosophers who came before him, beginning with the neo-Platonists, the "*nous*" is not a substance which resides "somewhere" as a *separate* substance, for in that case it would exist in space and time, and thus be finite. In Ferrarin's interpretation of Hegel, "The productive *nous* is nowhere other than in thinking, because it is nothing other than thinking; and thinking, irreducible to the thinker or to the psychological conditions for thought, can be said to be separate from them."[65] The "divine" for Hegel is the Concept as subject and as substance. The negativity of "feeling a lack" (the partial nonbeing of privation) is internal to the organism, but "a being which is capable of containing and enduring its own contradiction is a subject; that constitutes its infinity"; and in nature the living subject alone is the "concept; the unity of itself and its specific opposite."[66]

"Wonders are many, and none is more wonderful than man; nothing destined to befall him finds him without resources." So goes the quote on the first page of Hegel's *Philosophy of Nature* from Sophocles' *Antigone.* For Aristotle, the wonder of "man" is that he values *L ife*, whereas animals "just live." Hegel, in his reading of Aristotle, sees *entelechy* as that, in nature, "which produces itself," and sees *energeia* (translated as "actuality," "activity," "actuosity," "development" and "being at work") as the "actualization of a potency originally immanent in the subject of the process or movement."[67] For Hegel, the totality of self-actualizing processes accounts for the emergence of *subjectivity* in nature. The "final truth" of organic life is that the individual is inadequate to its genus, for which it is merely an instrument for perpetuation of the species. Within the objectification of self in the universal medium of reality, the human can assimilate nature as a moment of "ideal life" (rather than "bad infinity") and make individuality part and parcel of spirit's history. Ferrarin sees Hegel's sublation of nature in the *Philosophy of Spirit* as the realization that, "I am not tied to my biological life; I have a life, which means I am free from it (for example I can risk it for the sake of something higher)... It is self-consciousness and is thus divine. Its mortality is the mirror of the possibility of being immortal."[68]

The happiness of a good life, for Aristotle, spans a lifetime. As Ferrarin summarizes, "it is the exercise of a permanent possession, not a movement that ceases once it has reached its end; it is a being not a search, an actuality and not a result. . . It is complete at each moment and its end is its activity itself."[69] For Aristotle, the condition for happiness is the well-functioning polis, and the *material* principle of the polis is justice. This principle is defined as the quality and quantity of the citizens running their *oikoi* rather than the physical territory. The *active* principle of the polis is the legislator whose work founds the constitution and gives the polis its true *form*. The final purpose (*telos*) of the polis is self-sufficiency and the good life.[70] In Aristotle's *Politics*, the women and slaves of the *oikoi* and the barbarians outside of the polis represent a pre-political world ruled by the "passions" which need to be subjugated by men whose "superior" nature has been demonstrated by their actual creation of the polis. Aristotle makes a tripartition of the activities of the human community of the polis into *theoria* (theory and philosophy), *praxis* (action or activity) and *poiesis* (production). While *theoria* and *praxis* are activities with no other end than themselves, *poiesis*, as production performed by slaves, women, artisans and others excluded from citizenship, has its end outside of itself.

7 – COMMUNITY AND CIVIL SOCIETY

Ferrarin makes the point that Hegel's understanding of economics led him to recognize that in civil society the Aristotelian-Thomist motto "work-follows-being" is reversed. No longer is production subordinate to praxis or moral order; no longer does production, as *techne,* just imitate nature. From now on production is there to "liberate" us *from* nature and our perceived (or imagined) *human* nature. The dramatic change in mankind's relation to nature that takes place in modernity goes hand-in-hand with the post-Newtonian redefinition of science and philosophy. Ferrarin says that, although Hegel doesn't go the way of Descartes and Hobbes on this redefinition, which tends towards instrumental reason, he does seem to dissolve the Aristotelian tripartition of theory/activity/production: "production and activity become two sides of spirit's historical self-objectification that are united in the concept of work." In Antiquity the whole of the slave's activity belongs to the master, but in the modern mechanized world, for Hegel (in Ferrarin's interpretation), "Work is a self-externalization—that is, we do not transfer a form alien to ourselves, an *eidos* or *morphe* independent of us, onto external matter, we externalize ourselves."[71] The slave of Antiquity might assume the "form" of a farmer to work the master's land, but remains in "essence" for the master not a farmer but a slave (or "talking tool," to use Aristotle's chilling term); there is no pretense of liberty or equality or rights. Contrastingly, in capitalism the "free" individual enters the factory and sells his or her labor-power for an agreed wage, but in doing so *becomes*, according to Marx, a wage-slave.

The saving grace of modern civil society is for Hegel the freedom of the human *will*, a concept that only entered philosophy during the late Roman Empire with the Christianization of Neo-Platonism (or the Platonization of Christianity). Ferrarin says that for Hegel, "Freedom is not just an attribute of the will but its very nature, just as gravity is the nature of a body." Because the ego can negate its immediate desires by mediation of the tool it can willfully distance itself from nature and thus make nature into its own product. The exercise of free will in satisfying unitary needs through labor educates human impulses and brings about the rationalization of nature. Individuals want their externalized labor to be "recognized" in a universal system of needs. This self-affirmation by individuals initiates "a series of effects in the world which . . . will acquire a life of their own and get out of their control"; although, by the same token, as producers, "we are not bound to identify ourselves with the product."[72] By introducing the idea of freedom into production through the will, Ferrarin comments, "Hegel obviously obliterates the Aristotelian distinction between action and production."[73] Of this production-as-praxis, Hegel writes:

> The labour of the individual for his own wants is just as much a satisfaction of those of others as of himself, and the satisfaction of his work he attains only by the labour of others. As the individual in his own particular work ipso facto accomplishes unconsciously a universal work, so again he also performs the universal task as his conscious object. The whole becomes in its entirety his work, for which he sacrifices himself and precisely by that means receives back his own self from it.[74]

Following Kant, Hegel discerns the dualisms in civil society. Hegel is aware that there can be no restoration of the "organic unity" of the Greek World. But the recollection and understanding of what has been lost helps guard against illusions about what has been gained. In Hegel's view what makes the modern state different from the polis is that the system of needs constituted as civil society is estranged from the spiritual and political world. This modern dichotomy is further explored by the young Marx in *On the Jewish Question*. Marx says that the "political revolution," in smashing feudal institutions which had been "manifestations of the separation of the people from the community," thereby split society into, on the one hand, *individuals,* and on the other hand, the elements constituting the content of their lives and positions in society, which are themselves split between the *material* and the *spiritual*:

> A person's *particular* activity and situation in life sank to the level of purely individual significance. They no longer constitute the relationship of the individual to the state as a whole. Public affairs as such became the universal affair of each individual, and the political function became his universal function. But, the perfection of the idealism of the state is at the same time the perfection of the materialism of civil society. The shaking-off of the political yoke was at the same time the shaking-off of the bonds which had held in check the egoistic spirit of civil society. Political emancipation was, at the same time, the emancipation of civil society from politics, from even the *appearance* of a universal content.[75]

In Gillian Rose's interpretation Marx here exposes the "breaking of the middle." The guilds, statuses and privileges, which determined the rights and duties of individuals, formed the legal estate in the "middle" of the old feudal order. With the sweeping away of these institutions, the post-feudal individual is "naturalized as 'egoism' and allegorized as 'ethical.'"[76]

8 – KANT AND THE "AUTONOMOUS INTELLECT"

Having reached the crisis of civil society in the modern world of bourgeois revolutions, it is time to return to Sohn-Rethel and his analysis of the antithesis between mental and manual labor in class-divided societies. Sohn-Rethel describes how, ever since Antiquity, the "autonomous intellect" has been the "arsenal" from which intellectual labor draws its conceptual resources in order to dominate manual labor. After the decline of slavery in the Roman Empire and the ensuing growth of feudalism, a "personal unity of head and hand" emerges in medieval handicraft. In the new urban communities of the fifteenth and sixteenth centuries the artisan works not through abstract knowledge, but by practical know-how and manual expertise. Innovations in production stretch the capacities of the artisans, and from their ranks emerge the great artists, architects and engineers. But, in the Renaissance, Galilean science establishes the clear-cut division between head and hand.[77] The main qualification which the artisans lack for solving the problems facing them is mathematics: the "logic of socialized thought" which provides "the intellectual powers of social production." Sohn-Rethel writes: "It is no exaggeration to say that one can measure the extent of division of head and hand by the inroad of mathematics in any particular task."[78]

Newton, in redefining the astronomy of Kepler and Galileo, establishes a new science that identifies which forces hold the universe in place. Although Newton cannot explain the nature of these active forces, he can describe their laws in precise mathematical, quantitative terms. The possibilities of pure mathematics and pure science, as developed by Newton, are identified by Kant. In establishing how a priori judgments are possible, Kant separates a posterior and a priori principles, and separates mental and manual labor in a way which corresponds to this scientific method. According to Sohn-Rethel:

> Scientific experiment is often misinterpreted as an activity of manual labor complementing the intellectual labor of the mathematical hypotheses to be tested. But in fact the experiment is constructed to reduce the individual action to little more than reading the data from the instruments.[79]

Sohn-Rethel's analysis recalls Lukács' view on Kantian epistemology. In *History and Class Consciousness* (1923), Lukács challenges Engels' view that in Kant's epistemology the problem of the thing-in-itself is a barrier to concrete expansion of knowledge. Lukács writes:

> On the contrary, Kant, who sets out from the most advanced natural science of the day, namely from Newton's astronomy, tailors his theory of knowledge precisely to this science and its future potential.[80]

Science, confined to the Kantian world of phenomena and appearance is capable of limitless expansion through the autonomous intellect. Sohn-Rethel writes:

> Inertial motion such as Galileo applies in his research is in empty space and strictly rectilinear, which makes it unmistakably nonempirical... The immediate successors to Galileo, Descartes and Torricelli, are quite clear on the non-empirical character of Galileo's novel dynamic principle. Newton gave it the final acknowledgment under the name of 'the first law of motion'.[81]

Kant breaks open what Sohn-Rethel calls the "particular epistemological riddle of exact science": how non-empirical concepts can bear the necessary reference to nature. Kant, in grappling with the rational metaphysics of the eighteenth century, was shaken from his "slumbers" by David Hume's attack on metaphysics in *An Inquiry Concerning Human Understanding,*

> If we take in our hand any volume of divinity or school metaphysics, for instance let us ask, Does it contain any abstract reasoning concerning quantity or number? No. Does it contain any experimental reasoning concerning matter of fact and existence? No. Commit it then to the flames for it can contain nothing but sophistry and illusion.[82]

Hume's critique of metaphysics is accepted by Kant as a decisive refutation of the idea that the universal forms and categories of reason can be grounded by means of inductive logic in the external world as experienced through the senses. But Kant then turns the table on the empiricists with his argument that the universals are *a priori* to sensuous experience. Kant's *Critique of Pure Reason* explains that, in our perception of phenomena we find various contents, some experienced as external, some as internal. All of these experiences are subjective, but within them Kant finds a universal element—an a priori Other—which consists of the intuited sensible forms of Space and Time. The categories of the Understanding—including causality, universality and substantiality—are likewise a priori products of the universalizing mental structure. Though we are conscious of being determined by things happening outside of us, the pure, abstract principles of space and time enable us to perceive objects as separate from one another and events as succeeding one another. The a priori categories of transcendental logic enable us to make judgments about what is perceived. Though transcendental Kant's philosophy is not transcendent. Kant doesn't think that philosophy can transcend its own sphere to show the true reality of the thing-in-itself. Since scientific knowledge depends on concepts a priori *not* depicting nature as it really is, we can only understand nature as it corresponds to the concepts.[83] Reason is regulative, not constitutive; the understanding orders the objects as concepts and gives them unity so they can be applied practically. In Sohn-Rethel's interpretation, "the nature from which the nonempirical categories of intellectual labor are drawn is not the primary nature of physical reality but the second, purely social nature."[84] In effect Kant isolates that part of our being which can perform in separation from manual labor.

The Kantian experience is thus grounded in synthetic unity "according to concepts of objects of appearance." What is "objective" is only as it *appears* to the perceiving subject. But, as Kant does not wish to leave the individual subject stranded between frozen impersonal abstractions and the phenomenal world, he tries to actualize the human subject by attributing the fundamental principle of experience to a "transcendental spontaneity" of the mind in which the pure forms of intuition and understanding are constituted as the *activity* of pure apperception. In self-consciousness, the "I think" of the individual is posited as "my own" experience and as socialized through the intellectual labor of the understanding.[85] Sohn-Rethel agrees with Kant on the a priori origin of "the basic constituents of our form of cognition," but he doesn't attribute the a priori to a transcendental spontaneity of the mind. Rather, Sohn-Rethel sees the transcendental unity of self-consciousness as an intellectual reflection of the a priori form of social synthesis constituted and activated by the exchangeability of commodities through money.[86]

According to Sohn-Rethel, the exchange abstraction that produces the *form* of value, allows for and requires the actualization of intellectual labor as an a priori socialized form of thinking. In contrast, manual labor, which produces the *magnitude* of value, is reduced to an a priori *de*-socialized form of individual, "private" activity dependent on exchange relations.[87] Here Sohn-Rethel connects with Marx's analysis of how capital organizes and expands cooperation in production. The alienation of "private labors" takes place historically because the artisan is transformed into a factory hand, and takes place "logically" because, within capitalist production, the private individual who has to sell her labor power is isolated in her immediacy and forced into competition with other sellers of labor-power producing the same goods elsewhere. Kant argues that science, left unimpeded by religious and feudal institutions, serves the "natural" division between the educated and laboring classes—a view which is essentially the "backward" German version of the division between capital and labor in English political economy. Sohn-Rethel speculates that Adam Smith, if asked the question "how is social synthesis possible by means of commodity exchange?" might answer with the claim that humans produce and exchange commodities by their nature, and that class divisions are natural; thus social synthesis is achievable if the economy is unimpeded by feudal and religious restrictions on rights of property and trade.[88]

9 – CAPITALISM: DE-SOCIALIZED LABOR

According to Gillian Rose, on the "mature" writings of Marx in *Capital*,

> The theory of commodity fetishism is the most speculative moment in Marx's exposition of capital. It comes nearest to demonstrating in the historically specific case of commodity-producing society how substance is (mis)represented as subject, how necessary illusion arises out of productive activity.[89]

In contrast to this view of commodity-producing society as historically specific, Sohn-Rethel, in his essay "The Historical Materialist Theory of Knowledge," quotes and agrees with Thomson's argument that:

> civilized thought has been dominated from the earliest times down to the present day by what Marx called the fetishism of commodities, that is, the false consciousness generated by the social relations of commodity production. In early Greek philosophy we see this "false consciousness" gradually emerging and imposing on the world categories of thought derived from commodity production, as though these categories belonged, not to society, but to nature.[90]

Thus, in the Sohn-Rethel/Thomson thesis, the categories of Greek philosophy are seen as emerging from a "commodity fetishism" which is equated with the "false consciousness" or "practical solipsism" generated by money-mediated exchange. Sohn-Rethel sees Marx's *Capital* as, "in the first instance," a critique of political economy as "a particular mode of consciousness," employing such concepts employed by political economists as rent, profit, value and capital. Marx, in Sohn-Rethel's view, offers a critique of "thoughts, not things." Furthermore, Sohn-Rethel claims that Marx "does not elaborate concepts of his own, which as 'correct' ones, he would oppose to the false ones of the economists." But here Sohn-Rethel ignores what Marx regarded as his *original* conceptual contribution to the critique of political economy, namely the concept of the "dual character of labor": concrete and abstract. All labor in capitalism—and only in capitalism—is simultaneously the concrete exertion of particular labors and undifferentiated, abstract labor. As Marx puts it as early as 1844, capital is the expression of a special kind of work, indifferent to its content. Capital is also the expression of a being-for-self, abstracted from all other being, and produces humanity's dependence on a "very one-sided, machine-like labor."[91] In *Capital,* Marx refers to this original contribution of his as "the pivot on which a clear comprehension of political economy turns."[92] Although Sohn-Rethel recognizes that the human labor that has gone into production of commodities determines the magnitude of their value, he argues,

> The abstraction does not spring from labour but from exchange as a particular mode of social interrelationship, and it is through exchange that the abstraction imparts itself to labour, making it "abstract human labour." [93]

The fact that commodity-exchange existed in Antiquity does not mean that the "false consciousness" arising from it was universally fetishistic in anything like the modern sense. To quote Marx on Aristotle's groping towards a concept of "equivalent form,"

> Aristotle therefore himself tells us what prevented any further analysis: the concept of value. What is the homogenous element, i.e., the common substance, which the house represents from the point of view of the bed, in the value expression for the bed? Such a thing, in truth, cannot exist for Aristotle.[94]

Marx says that Aristotle was unable to see that what was really equal, between the bed and the house, was human labor:

> The secret of the expression of value, namely the quality and equivalence of all kinds of labour because and in so far as they are human labour in general, could not be deciphered until the concept of human equality had already acquired the permanence of fixed popular opinion. This however only becomes possible in a society where the commodity form is the universal form of the product of labour hence the dominant social relation is the relation between men as possessors of commodities.[95]

Marx, in his "Notes on Adolf Wagner," is quite clear that in *Capital* his investigation of the commodity, as the "simplest social form in which the product of labor in contemporary society manifests itself," is "historically specific." [96] That Marx's theory of commodity fetishism is not transhistorical and therefore cannot be "applied" to Greek Antiquity might help to explain why Marx, in the third volume of *Capital*, says that in the Greek polis, as in primitive communism, it is the "actual community and its conditions that presents itself as the basis of production... its reproduction of this community being production's final purpose." The relations of production in the polis—a class-divided society of appropriation in Sohn-Rethel's terms—are contrasted, not only with feudalism—where the forms of domination appear openly as the "motive power" of feudal servitude—but also with capitalism, which is characterized by "economic mystification."[97] Marx's use of the terms "community" and "final purpose" indicates that he is engaging with

Aristotle's view on the teleological relation of praxis and production in the polis. In investigating how necessary illusion arises out of productive activity in capitalism, Marx appears to be revisiting Hegel's *Philosophy of Spirit*, which sums up the dialectic of freedom and necessity as "finding a world presupposed before us, generating a world as our own creation, and gaining freedom from it and in it."[98]

Marx conceives of a possible post-capitalist society, in which rational governance by the "associated producers" would form the basis for a "realm of freedom." This realm, he adds, "really begins only where labor determined by necessity and external expediency ends."[99] Marx's critical appropriation (through Hegel) of Aristotle's idea of the "realm of freedom" also emerges in his *Critique of the Gotha Program* with the observation that the higher phase of socialism/communism would abolish the antithesis between mental and physical labor characteristic of class society.

Sohn-Rethel says that the "logic of appropriation" cannot change into a "logic of production" until *de*-socialized labor is *re*-socialized and "people create their own society as producers."[100] The problem is that he thinks the only thing preventing social labor from becoming *directly* socialized is the exchange relation; a society is potentially classless when it acquires the form of its synthesis "directly through the process of production and not through exchange-mediated appropriation."[101] As Moishe Postone has observed, the mode of societalization effected by industrial labor is positively evaluated by Sohn-Rethel as non-capitalist and opposed to the mode effected by exchange, which is assessed as the essence of capitalism. Postone sees in this claim the error of restricting abstraction to "a market phenomenon completely extrinsic to labor in capitalism." To restrict the value-form to the abstraction in exchange is to ignore abstract labor as forming the basis for alienated social structures.[102]

In the alienated social structures of the USSR—a "society of production" and of "socialized labor" in Sohn-Rethel's terms, whatever his criticisms of it—Stalin's political economists claimed that the contradiction between private and social labor had been resolved because the State Plan had superseded exchange-mediated appropriation, even though class inequalities—between managers and managed; between intellectual and manual laborpersisted. The fact that money and value mediated the quantitative relationship of this inequality did not, as far as Stalinist ideology was concerned, stop labor from being directly, or immediately, "social." Thus, even though the quantity of labor was measured as quantity of output rather than hours of labor-time, and even though goods were being produced without having to be sold on the market, unequal exchange of labors was maintained—mediated by the planners and administrators of state-capitalism—and passed off as "socialism."[103]

Sohn-Rethel was doubtless highly critical of the divisions and inequalities in the "socialist" economy between mental and manual workers. Note his insistence that, "to the conditions of a classless society we must add, in agreement with Marx, the unity of mental and manual labor, or as he puts it, the disappearance of their division." But this goal is never grounded in Sohn-Rethel's critique. His statement to the effect that the struggle against the division between intellectual and manual labor had formed "a central issue in the construction of socialism in China since the victory of the proletarian cultural revolution" betrays a Kantian dualism between "ought" and "is," if not a lapse into Maoist voluntarism.[104] This is not to say that Sohn-Rethel's ideas can be reduced to Stalinist Diamat or Maoism. His materialism differentiates itself from communist orthodoxy by asserting that the reality Marx opposes to forms of consciousness is not "matter" but social existence:

> The reality, then to which Marx critically opposes the various forms of consciousness of men is the historical one of their own social existence. It is not 'matter'; or the 'external world material world independent of consciousness'. Our notions of things and the concepts in which we undertake their systematization are historical products themselves. So are science, mathematics, natural philosophy. It is for the historical materialist to account for the rise as well as the objective validity of science in history, not for the logic of natural science as a logic reflected from nature to supply the principles of historical materialism.[105]

In "The Historical Materialist Theory of Knowledge," Sohn-Rethel notes that categories such as substance, being, magnitude, abstract time and space, and uniform movement are similar to the "principles of being" discussed in Engels' *Anti-Dühring.* Engels asks, "Whence does thought obtain these principles?" He answers:

> From itself? No. . . the realm of pure thought is limited to logical schemata... but what we are dealing with here are forms of being, of the external world, and these forms can never be created and derived by thought out of itself, but only from the external world. But with this the whole relationship is inverted: the principles are not the starting point of the investigation, but its final result; they are not applied to Nature and human history, but abstracted from them; it is not Nature and the realm of humanity which conform to these principles, but the principles are only valid in so far as they are in conformity with Nature and history. That is the only materialistic conception of the matter.[106]

Sohn-Rethel points out that Engels' formulations were further developed by Lenin for his "theory of reflection" in *Materialism and Empirio-Criticism.* Sohn-Rethel concedes that there seems to be "at first sight, a certain incompatibility" between his own view, that the basic principles of knowledge can be traced to a root in "social existence," and the view that they can be derived from the external world by way of abstraction and reflection.[107] In proposing a reconciliation, Sohn-Rethel argues that he is opposing the idealism of the Kantian transcendental synthesis by means of a materialist "critique of epistemology." But his "methodological postulate" nevertheless employs a neo-Kantian turn: having presupposed the object of his critique—a norm of "objectively deceptive" universal logic, locked in the "false consciousness of timelessness"—he then seeks to discover the conditions of its possibility in the "social synthesis" established in the ancient world through exchange value facilitated by invention of coined money.

Because his "solution" involves a "methodological postulate" it needs to be compared with the use of "postulate" in Kantian and neo-Kantian method. In Kant's *Critique of Pure Reason*, "objective validity" is restricted to the conditions of the possibility of objects of experience through appearances, and, more generally, the conditions of all knowledge of objects. Empirical knowledge is made possible in the synthesis of perceptions and objects of experience with general, a priori rules. Neo-Kantian sociology seeks to develop a scientific method for investigating the sphere of moral facts and values, the objective validity of which is conferred by the power of society or culture. But a sociological a priori, unlike Kant's transcendental unity of apperception, is external to the mind, and therefore has an object-like, causal relationship to thinking.[108] Durkheim, seeking to discover the social conditions of the possibility of actual experiences in human communities and of their objective validity, locates the origin of moral or coercive force in "collective consciousness" (or "collective being"), acting as a sui generis, underivable "transcendent objectivity." But because of its transcendent and underivable nature, this precondition cannot be a "fact" itself; therefore it is—like God or Freedom in Kant's practical reason, which is introduced to make morality intelligible—a *postulate*. The difference, as Rose points out, is that for Kant the postulate is only regulative, whereas for Durkheim it is constitutive. The similarity is that in both cases the postulates—God and collective consciousness—are what makes social experience possible or intelligible, even though what is postulated, in both cases, remains unknowable and unanalyzable. Rose argues that once the social origin of the categories is admitted it becomes impossible to explain the relation between the unconditioned and conditioned without using the very categories of the conditioned (such as cause) which need to be justified by the precondition.[109]

Does Sohn-Rethel's "methodological postulate" escape the horns of this apparent logical dilemma? As we have seen, Sohn-Rethel aims to replace the Kantian transcendental unity of consciousness with his methodological postulate of the social synthesis brought about by commodity-exchange, of which the "objectively false consciousness" of idealist philosophical thinking is a reflex or projection. In reference to the historical developments in Greek antiquity, Sohn-Rethel highlights the triumph of the ideology of philosophical idealism in "class struggle" against a "scientific" form of "materialism" representative of the "practical" artisans of the "lower orders." Sohn-Rethel and Thomson believed that early Greek "science" had already established the categories of analysis, such as cause. Therefore, if this assessment of a putative materialism in pre-Socratic thought (rendered dormant until its renovation by Marxian materialism) is sound, then the apparent incompatibility—between Sohn-Rethel's tracing the basic principles of knowledge to a root in "social existence" and Diamat's deriving of the principles from the external world by way of abstraction and reflection—would seem to be overcome. But the reconciliation between his methodological postulate and Engelsian reflection theory rests on a questionable historical validation. What Seaford discerns in the work of Thomson as a tendency towards "reductionism" and "dogmatism" can be seen in the latter's attempt, not only to divide Greek philosophy into "idealism" and "materialism" in the tradition of Engels, but also to reduce the divide to *contending social classes*. According to Thomson's communist colleague, Benjamin Farrington (1891–1974)—whose writings on Greece are quoted favorably, and at length, by Sohn-Rethel—a "secular" scientific movement began in the sixth century BCE among the Greeks. Starting with Thales, then Anaximander, then Epicurus, this movement "offered a general explanation of nature without invoking the aid of any power outside nature." Farrington claims that the atomistic philosophy of Epicurus was scientifically true, potentially useful for material progress, and philanthropic as a popular philosophy. Farrington asserts that "the kind of things that Anaximander was saying in his book *On Nature* were the same kind of things that an up-to-date writer puts forward to-day in a scientific handbook of the universe"; and that Anaximander drew his conclusions about the universe from observation and reflection. These claims, which Farrington published in 1936, were challenged at the outset by Cornford, who had argued in *From Religion to Philosophy* (published in 1912) that although the Milesian philosophers structured their abstract schemes of conception on the basis of the intuitive certainties of geometry, they were not, as some have imagined, "scientists" in any later sense of the word, i.e., they were not dispassionate observers taking in and explaining sensory data with theoretical hypotheses. Cornford, in a forgotten essay of 1941 entitled "The Marxist View of Ancient Philosophy," comments:

> What sort of observation could have taught Anaximander that the earth is a cylindrical drum, three times as broad as it is high; or that the fixed stars, the moon, and the sun, in that order, are respectively distant from the earth by 9, 18, and 27 times the diameter of the earth?

Cornford goes on to challenge Farrington and Thomson's view of "materialism" as "frowned upon by the ruling class as subversive":

> I venture to say that no spectator, listening to Prometheus' recital of the arts bestowed on man to alleviate his miserable condition, could possibly have associated those arts with the atomic theory or with any Ionian system... Prometheus is called by Mr Thomson 'the patron saint of the proletariat', and the proletariat of antiquity were, he tells us, the slave population. But it was not an audience of slaves, or of workers or peasants, that met in the house of the wealthy Callias to hear the great sophists, Protagoras, Hippias, and Prodicus.

Farrington argues that "primitive materialism" was the emancipatory ideology of the "little people" in the struggle against the idealism of Plato, who wished to deny them access to truth and "poison their minds with outworn superstitions." Thomson, for his part, claims that following the Peloponnesian War, Athenian thought was divided between those who supported the city-state (who were rich, such as Plato) and those who were prepared to see it fall (who were not rich). Cornford comments, "The implication that the abolition of the city-state would have entailed the abolition of social inequalities, including slavery, is hard to justify in the light of history."[110]

10 – ABSOLUTE NEGATIVITY AS ANTI-CAPITALISM

Can Sohn-Rethel's neo-Kantian critique of Greek philosophy be justified in the more modern light of the philosophical struggle between Kant and Hegel, and its implications for Marx's critique of capital? Georg Lukács, writing in the section on the "Antinomies of Bourgeois Thought" in his essay "Reification and the Consciousness of the Proletariat," says that the critical (Kantian) philosophy springs from the reified structure of consciousness in the modern world. In contrast, the problems and solutions of Ancient Greek philosophy, embedded in a wholly different society, were qualitatively different from those of modern philosophy:

> Greek philosophy was no stranger to certain aspects of reification, without having experienced them, however, as universal forms of existence; it had one foot in the world of reification while the other remained in a 'natural' society.[111]

In his later book, *The Young Hegel* (1936), Lukács shows how Hegel's early admiration for the organic "wholeness" of Greek Antiquity stemmed from his contempt for the dogmatic, anti-philosophical philistinism he saw in contemporary Christianity, which Lukács refers to as "the survival of medieval narrowness in the life and thought of modern time."[112] Furthermore, "Hegel's enthusiasm for the classical democracies was interwoven with his attitude to the French Revolution"—an attitude that was similarly enthusiastic. Lukács says that, although the young Hegel disregarded the existence of slavery in Antiquity, his concept of the classical democracies was "essentially classless": "As soon as class distinctions became economically and politically fixed, real freedom was at an end."[113] By 1805, Hegel, having developed a perspective on history influenced by his economic studies, had abandoned his youthful dream of the revolutionary revival of classical civilization. According to Lukács, in Hegel's new view of history the dissolution of the classical city-states was not merely "historically necessary"; from the ruins, a higher social principle had emerged. In the Platonic republic, in Hegel's words, "the absolute self-knowledge of the individual did not yet exist, this absolute being-in oneself was not present... Plato did not set up an ideal, he interiorized the state of his age within himself. But this state has perished—the Platonic republic is not realizable... because it lacked the principle of absolute individuality."[114]

Hegel, in tracing the Idea of Freedom, refers to the principle of absolute individuality as the historical contribution of Christianity. In asserting the absolute independence of human personality, the Christian religion paved the way for philosophical enquiries into the faculty of cognition, the opposition of subject and object, and the personality's existence in and for itself:

> The Athenian, the Roman, knew he was free. But that man, as such, is free—as a human being, is born free—was unknown to Plato and to Aristotle, to Cicero and to the Roman jurists, although this conception alone is the source of all jurisprudence. In Christianity we find, for the first time, the individual personal soul depicted as possessing an infinite, absolute value. . . These modes of representation make freedom independent of rank, birth, cultivation and the like; and the progress which has been made by this means is immense. Yet this mode of viewing the matter is somewhat different from the fact that freedom is an indispensable element in the conception—man. The undefined feeling of this fact has worked for centuries in the dark; the instinct for freedom had produced the most terrible revolutions, but the idea of the innate freedom of man—this knowledge of his own nature—is not old.[115]

Sohn-Rethel, not wishing to engage with the Hegelian dialectic, writes, "I have never felt convinced that to advance from the critical idealism of Kant to the critical materialism of Marx the road should necessarily lead via the absolute idealism of Hegel."[116] Chris Arthur, who argues, in similar terms to Sohn-Rethel's, that labor only becomes abstract in exchange, asks, "cannot we employ the Marxian insight into the relation of social being and social consciousness in a critique of Hegel's dialectic?" Arthur writes:

> Strangely, Sohn-Rethel did not take the next step, which is to grasp the self-differentiating, self-developing, and self-synthesizing Absolute of Hegel as the ideological expression of the rule of capital. There is more than a Weberian 'elective affinity' between the self-movement of thought in the *Logic* and M-C-M [money-commodities-more money]. The great difficulty capital has in

> passing from the sphere of frictionless circulation, where it is at home with itself, to production, where it has to grapple with its "other," where it gets bogged down in the finitude of rusting machinery and striking labourers—all this is paralleled in the difficulty Hegel has in giving an account of how the logical forms go over to the real world.[117]

Leaving aside, for the moment, "the difficulty Hegel has in giving an account of how the logical forms go over to the real world," we might note that there is, in fact, a discernible affinity between Marx's critique of the political economists' explications of the labor theory of value and Hegel's critique of the Kantian transcendental subject. For Hegel argues that in the opposition of form and content, the content is not formless. To regard form as something external in relation to content is a Kantian error. As Isaak Rubin observes:

> From the standpoint of Hegelian philosophy… the content itself in its development gives birth to this form, which was contained within this content in concealed form.… From this standpoint, the form of value also must arise of necessity from the substance of value, and consequently we must view abstract labor as the substance of value, in all the fullness of its social features which are characteristic for commodity production.[118]

Dunayevskaya's 1949 essay, "Notes on Chapter One of Marx's *Capital* in relation to Hegel's *Logic*," seems to concur with Rubin on this issue: the "illusory" nature of the commodity fetish cannot be overcome by simply counterposing essence (concrete, "useful" labor conceived as the source of all value) to form (appearance of exchange-values as phenomena and phantasmagoria). For to do so would fail to comprehend their interpenetration and opposition in a single commodity acting as an equivalent. In this phantasmagoria, use-value becomes the phenomenal form of its opposite, *value*. Concrete labor becomes the mere matter of the form under which abstract labor manifests itself. Private labors are socialized by the general value-form. The general value-form allows for, and requires, the existence of the money-form.[119] Marx likens the general form that money assumes as the equivalent commodity to Plato's ideal forms:

> It is as if alongside and external to lions, tigers, rabbits, and all other actual animals, which form when grouped together the various kinds, species, subspecies, families etc., of the animal kingdom, there existed also in addition *the animal*, the individual incarnation of the entire animal kingdom.[120]

The general value-form reduces all actual labor to the expenditure of *labor-power* —in a bad infinity of unlimited "growth" and accumulation of capital. Under the thumb of capital, labor is substance, not subject. Labor is not actualized as subject in a conflict between "good" use-value and "bad" exchange-value. "Labor," as the proletariat, only becomes a "subject" in its self-abolition and uprooting of value-production. Marx says, "The life-process of society . . . does not strip off its mystical veil until it is treated as production by freely associated men, and is consciously regulated by them according to a settled plan." [121] Dunayevskaya comments:

> Until then the *differentia specifica* of the value-form remains a secret even to a Ricardo, just as much as the *equivalent* form remained a secret even to an Aristotle who lived in Greek society founded on slavery. How could it be otherwise when the most unnatural and fantastic form of all – *the commodity form of labor*, labor power—is accepted by this society as a matter of course? [emphases in original] [122]

Peter Hudis suggests (in a critique of Postone), that even if we grant that Hegel's *Logic* represents the logic of capital, it does not necessarily follow that Hegel's philosophy represents the value-form:

> The logic of capital presents us with a system imbued with such internal instability that capital intimates a realm beyond capital wherein [in Marx's words, echoing Aristotle's] "human power is its own end." Likewise, Hegel's *Logic* is traversed by an internal duality: the absolute contradiction between the Theoretical and Practical Idea. [123]

The internal duality of Hegel's *Logic* is explored by Herbert Marcuse in his early work, *Hegel's Ontology and the Theory of Historicity* (1932). Contrary to Arthur's view of Hegel's Logic as a "self-differentiating, self-developing, and self-synthesizing" road to the absolute, for Marcuse *all three* parts of Hegel's *Logic* (Being, Essence and Concept) are pervaded with difference and differences. As the category of being is purely indeterminate and empty it is not any thing, and therefore is Nothing, which is *always* the absolute other of being. Even though the nothing of being can never have any presence in Life, it *constitutes* it. Being, in the sphere of immediacy, is the simple negativity of itself, a negativity which is the source of its movement in becoming. In the Doctrine of Essence, beings *mediate* their past with the present as a way of opening up their future, and existence is revealed as a presupposition which needs to be posited again as *actuality*. At every stage reality is found to be a "beyond," and particular forms of existence are found to contradict their content. Ultimately the forward movement of logical forms is comprehended as a *concrete* (and therefore differentiated) *totality*. [124]

In the realization of reason and the *Good* in the historical process, Hegel's Spirit unfolds itself in the world as the Notion (or Concept), transformed by desire and labor. Spirit has a "we-like" character, grounded in Life, the first form of the Idea in Hegel's Doctrine of the Concept. Life as spirit orients the meaning of being as a process which unifies the I with the world, and spirit with nature (here, nature includes human interactions with each other as well as with non-human beings and objects). The second form of the Idea is Cognition, which is subdivided into pure cognition and volition (there is no third term; Hegel here abandons the triadic form of presentation—thus indicating that it was *only* a form of presentation). Pure cognition has for its object the True; Volition, the active self-universalizing subject, has for its object the Good. Marcuse writes: "Is there a higher truth of life which does not suffer from the deficiency of cognition? Indeed this is the 'practical idea' of action, the Idea of the good." But, as Marcuse concludes, following Hegel's text very closely, the practical Idea is not ultimately higher than cognition; rather it is itself a *mode* of cognition.[125] Marcuse, who, in this early work, sees Hegel as the philosopher of the French Revolution, rather than the Restoration, writes:

> So long as the "good" to be realized through the practical Idea is considered a "subjective purpose" alone which is not implicitly contained in objective actuality but which first must be embedded in it, then action is just as deficient as knowledge, but in the opposite sense… Pure cognition [the Idea of the True] views its world as the other which is implicitly true, thereby misunderstanding the subjectivity of objectivity, whereas action [the Idea of the Good] treats the world as empty receptacle for the actualization of its subjective purposes, thereby misunderstanding the objectivity of subjectivity.[126]

In Hegel's words on the subjectivity-objectivity relation,

> When external actuality is altered by the activity of the objective notion and its determination therewith sublated, by that very fact the merely phenomenal reality, the external determinability and worthlessness, are removed from that actuality.[127]

The objective Other of the Idea is Nature, which prompts a return to considering "the difficulty Hegel has in giving an account of how the logical forms go over to the real world." The *Philosophy of Nature* , which in the *Encyclopedia* follows the *Logic* and precedes the *Philosophy of Spirit*, deals with chemistry, geology, botany and zoology, all as understood in the empirical sciences of the Enlightenment. Dieter Wandschneider suggests that, although Hegel's concept of nature doesn't represent an intuition of the now established fact of natural evolution, what does emerge at the end of his *Philosophy of Nature* is nonetheless the concept of "a being capable of thought." Wandschneider sees the relationship between Logic, Nature and Mind in Hegel's dialectic as working itself out through the mediation of "idealized nature or naturalized idea" in the form of "culture realized in a physical world."[128] Nature is portrayed as the "Other" of the Idea, but at the same time Hegel sees Nature as representing the Idea's essential freedom, as consummated in Hegel's *Science of Logic* in his discussion of the organic existence of "Life" as the teleological development of the thinking (social) subject. The self-determined idea of the Logic, once unfolded, "freely releases" Nature—as understood in all its diversity and objectivity. But in Nature, the logical does not itself generate the sequential categories; for subjectivity only comes at the end, in the concept of the telos. Nature, as the otherness of the Idea, finds its immediacy in the external dimension of space. But Hegel's further definition of the idea as nature is not a becoming or transition; it is a free resolution on the part of the Absolute Idea to let itself be in otherness. It is in this process of letting itself go as immediately existing being that Being "is and becomes."

John Burbidge, commenting on Popper's assertion that Hegel's dialectic was an attempt to "draw real physical rabbits out of purely metaphysical hats," points out that "a rabbit has its own independent life before the magician went on stage." Furthermore, "Hegel's magic comes not from producing something out of nothing, but from detailed reflection on the way the brute facts of existence acquire significance and meaning, even as our sense of meaning and significance organizes the way we read the facts of experience."[129]

In Lenin's 1914 "materialist" reading of Hegel's *Science of Logic* the Absolute Idea represents the unity of theory and practice through the will to *assimilate* nature. For Lenin, the Absolute Idea is the "objective truth" of the Notion (Concept); the Notion is "Man"; and "Man" is "in itself" its own Other, as "Nature independent of man."[130] In the context of his revolutionary perspective during World War One, Lenin's "objective truth" can be seen as the subjective-objective conditions for revolution. The "Nature independent of man," that is Man's own other, can be seen as the social and productive resources deemed necessary for building a new society. But, as Dunayevskaya puts it (reading Lenin reading Hegel), anyone looking for the end of contradictions in the Absolute Idea is in for "a real shocker," because Hegel tells us that "the Absolute Idea contains the highest opposition within itself," which necessitates further development within the concrete totality.[131]

In order to grasp what is at issue here, we must turn to what Ferrarin calls "one of the most important and overlooked 'meta-theories' of the *Encyclopedia*: the concluding three syllogisms."[132] At the end of Hegel's *Philosophy of Spirit* (the third part of his *Encyclopedia of Philosophical Sciences*) philosophy as absolute spirit "looks back" at itself as the result, not only of the preceding moments of art and religion, but also as the totality of the three parts of the *Encyclopedia*: logic, nature, and finite spirit. Logic, Nature and Mind/Spirit each form in turn the syllogisms of Universal-Particular-Individual. In the first syllogism, in which Logic forms the universal term, nature has been defined as a transition point and negative factor; yet it is also as "implicitly the Idea." Reinhart Maurer (whatever his intent) echoes Lenin in describing the mediation of Nature as a "turn" towards "Liberty," "Darwin . . . [and] dialectical materialism."[133] Hegel however, suggests that, if the progression of the *Encyclopedia* (Logic-Nature-Spirit) is syllogized *absolutely* as Universal-Particular-Individual, it is potentially misleading. Ferrarin explains:

> The transition from Idea to nature, then to spirit, or from the Idea in itself to Idea outside itself, then to the Idea returning to itself as spirit, is now characterized by Hegel as having been presented in the insufficient terms of the Logic of Being.[134]

The Doctrine of Being is the realm of immediacy which turns out be *essentially* to be "illusory being." The mediating role of nature in the syllogism Logic-Nature-Spirit does not in itself achieve the goal of philosophy as set out in Hegel's *Phenomenology:* a "knowledge [that] no longer needs to go beyond itself."[135] Ferrarin says that while the essence of the Theoretical Idea is to unveil Nature's true being in contemplation, the Practical Idea, whose essence is to assimilate externality, gives rise to the violent subjugation of nature-as-nonbeing. Ferrarin suggests that if we can realize Hegel's proposal to overcome this contradiction, then, "we will stop treating nature as an enemy to be colonized or as an externality to unveil. Rather, once nature is understood as a living whole and as a concept-in-itself, spirit will comprehend nature as its own inner foundation and at the same time put a limit to the bad infinity of its exploitation of nature through work."[136]

In the second syllogism of Absolute Spirit—Nature-Mind-Logic—finite Spirit/Mind presupposes Nature and couples itself with Logic: "Mind reflects on itself in the Idea: philosophy appears as subjective cognition, of which liberty is the aim, and which is itself the way to produce it."[137] Here, Maurer sees the mediation of Mind/Spirit as the philosophy of history represented by the *Phenomenology of Spirit.*[138] Similarly, Martin Heidegger argues that Marx's "metaphysics" of labor was "thought through beforehand" in Hegel's *Phenomenology of Spirit* "as the process of unconditional production setting itself up, that is, as the objectification of the real by human beings experienced as subjectivity." [139] The term "unconditional production" in fact resembles Marx's description of capitalist production as "production for production's sake," which is riven by the absolute contradiction between: 1) the drive to increase productivity by reducing the proportion of living labor and 2) the reproductive drive to increase surplus value, which is wholly dependent on living labor. Heidegger however, argues that unconditional production would only be further fortified by the triumph of the Hegelian-Marxist "unconditional self-assertion" of the "*subjectivity* of humanity as a totality."[140]

In the second syllogism Spirit is the middle that brings together nature and the Idea to science. According to Ferrarin, although "the presentation acquires the relational character of the Logic of Essence and is thus higher," it has the limitation of being the syllogism of mind/spirit in the appearance of science "as a human construct, a *subjective* cognition producing freedom and absolute knowledge."[141] This might suggest that it is "subjective" because the "science" is merely instrumental reason and the "freedom" is a bourgeois illusion. "Subjective cognition" might be taken as an attractive proposition to those over-burdened with worries about "dehumanizing the Idea." But in a less naïve sense it contains the possibility of a collapse back into a subjective construction along the lines of *homo faber* or even *homo oeconomicus*, and a collapse of *poiesis* into a *techne* based on the ever-intensifying exploitation of living labor and the infinite reduction of nature to nonbeing.

Dunayevskaya disagrees with Maurer's view that in the second syllogism the *Phenomenology of Spirit* represents the mediation of Mind/Spirit. She points out that Phenomenology, as set out in the *Philosophy of Spirit,* gets just a single section under Psychology.[142] Dunayevskaya, quoting Hegel on "subjective cognition . . . which is itself the way to produce it," comments, "I cannot help thinking of Marx concluding that the [Paris] Commune is 'the form at last discovered to work out the economic emancipation of the proletariat.'. . . Mind itself, the new society is 'the mediating agent in the process.'"[143] Dunayevskaya however, in her later writings, adds that unless Spirit, as essence, is united with something, "it's like asking someone suddenly to walk on his head." She connects Hegel's decision not to stop at Mind/Spirit as essence with his concerns that, following the havoc of the industrial and political revolutions, and Kant's "Copernican Revolution in thought," there was a danger of regression represented by Friedrich Jacobi's "irrationalism."

Jacobi argued that Reason could do no more than provide finite and quantitative knowledge about the conditions of existence. He further argued that conditioned existence presupposed an unconditioned which neither reason nor science could define or determine. Whereas for Kant faith was a postulate of practical reason for the solution of the contradiction between the World and the Ideal of the Good, for Jacobi any relation between the individual and the unconditioned could only be *immediate* knowledge gained through inward revelation.[144] Hegel argues that "the Christian faith is a copious body of objective truth, a system of knowledge and doctrine; while the scope of the philosophic faith [Jacobi] is so utterly indefinite, that, while it has room for the faith of the Christian, it equally admits belief in the divinity of the Dalai Lama, the ox, or the monkey."[145]

Hegel, writing in the *Science of Logic* on the identity of the theoretical and practical ideas in the absolute, at the same time claims that the Absolute Idea "contains within itself the highest degree of opposition"; furthermore it "possesses personality" which is nonetheless "not exclusive individuality, but explicitly universality and cognition."[146] Here Hegel invokes his historical description of Socrates as representing a dialectical unity of personality and individuality. But as Russell Rockwell points out, "Hegel's suggestion seems to be that whereas in ancient Greece there was one such personality (Socrates), contemporary historical conditions hold the potential to realize such 'personality' generally."[147]

As much as Socrates and Plato, Hegel invokes Aristotle. He does so when, following the syllogisms Logic-Nature-Mind and Nature-Mind-Logic, Hegel breaks the sequence and in the third syllogism *con*sequentially introduces the "Idea of philosophy." Here self-knowing reason divides itself into Spirit (Mind), as the presupposition of its subjective activity, and Nature, "as process of the objectively and implicitly existing idea." The Concept, as the thing-in-itself, moves and develops, yet is equally the action of cognition.[148] Hegel, having shown how civil society abolishes the Aristotelian tripartition of knowing, acting and making, finally seems to reunite them in the final words of the *Encyclopedia*: "The eternal Idea which is in itself and for itself actualizes, produces, and enjoys itself as absolute spirit." Here, Ferrarin says, "Hegel makes a strikingly un-Aristotelian identification of theoria, praxis, and poiesis (knowing, acting, making)."[149]

Dunayevskaya interprets Hegel's final words in the *Encyclopedia* as the philosophical projection of a "new society" and claims that in Marx the Idea's absolute negativity expresses his concept of "revolution in permanence," as well as the argument in the *Critique of the Gotha Program* that the "all-round development of the individual" requires the abolition of the "enslaving subordination" to the division of labor and of the antithesis between mental and manual labor.[150] Marx's *Critique of the Gotha Program* was of course not a program. As Dunayevskaya puts it:

> The whole truth is that even Marx's *Critique of the Gotha Program* , which remains the ground for organization today, was written 112 years ago. What is demanded is not mere "updating," after all the aborted revolutions of the post-World War II world. "Ground" will not suffice alone; we have to finish the building—the roof and its contents. [151]

For Sohn-Rethel too, the *Critique of the Gotha Program* was the "ground" for his main thesis, but he thought that the roof and contents of socialism could be built by suppressing the operation of exchange value, while the groundwork task of breaking down the division between mental and manual labor could be left to the contingencies of "revolutionary will." He did not see the organizational ground as philosophical as well as historical. As Adorno wrote (probably with Sohn-Rethel in mind):

> Metaphysical categories are not merely an ideology concealing the social system; at the same time they express its nature, the truth about it and in their changes are precipitated those of the most central experiences.[152]

And according to Marcuse, philosophy is,

> the scientific expression of a certain fundamental human attitude… toward being and beings in general, and through which a historical-social situation often can express itself more clearly and deeply than in the reified, practical spheres of life.[153]

As Rosa Luxemburg said, at the moment the Greeks entered history, their situation was that of a disintegrated primitive communism. In that case "communism" made its first appearance in *philosophy* amongst the elite of Plato's *Republic*, at the very time it was being extinguished, in its "primitive" forms, throughout the Greek World. The advent of coined money in Antiquity as "real abstraction" undoubtedly influenced the formulations of the philosophers; but so also did changes in class relationships, social practices and beliefs. In a more modern context, we have seen arguments relating the roles of money, exchange-value and capital to Kant's transcendental synthesis and to Hegel's "self-synthesizing" absolutes. But why should the importance of the Hegelian dialectic for interpreting Marx's critique of capitalism be restricted to consideration of Hegel's Logic as expressing the self-movement of the logic of capital? Hegel's *Logic*, even as it represents the logic of capital, is like all of his philosophy imbued with an absolute negativity, which can be read as anticipating Marx's critique of capital, in which the logic of the system intimates a realm beyond it. The claim that Hegel's philosophy is obsolete apart from its logical "method" blocks investigation into the relatively unexplored relation between Marx's concerns with theorizing an alternative to capitalism and the "absolute negativity" of Hegel's concept of freedom expressed in such works as the *Phenomenology of Spirit* and *Philosophy of Spirit.*

NOTES

1. Alfred Sohn-Rethel, *Intellectual and Manual Labour: A Critique of Epistemology* (London: Macmillan, 1976), p. xiii. Henceforth abbreviated as *"IML."*
2. Stefan Müller-Doohm, *Adorno: A Biography* (London: Polity, 2005), pp. 219–21; Peter Stirk, *Max Horkheimer: A New Interpretation* (Lanham, MD: Lexington Books, 1992), pp. 122–23.
3. Sohn-Rethel, *IML,* pp. x–xiv.
4. Sohn-Rethel, *IML,* p. 57.
5. Sohn-Rethel, *IML,* pp. 26–27.
6. Sohn-Rethel, *IML,* p. 42.
7. Sohn-Rethel, *IML,* p. 43, p. 99.
8. Sohn-Rethel, *IML,* pp. 46–49.

9. Sohn-Rethel, *IML,* pp. 3–4.
10. Sohn-Rethel, *IML,* pp. 88–94.
11. Francis Macdonald Cornford, *The Unwritten Philosophy* (Cambridge University Press: 1950), pp. 30–31.
12. George Thomson, *The First Philosophers: Studies in Ancient Greek Society* (London: Lawrence and Wishart, 1955), p. 228.
13. Thomson, *The First Philosophers,* p. 219; Hegel, *Lectures in the History of Philosophy I*, ch. I, pt. A (2).
14. Francis Macdonald Cornford, *From Religion to Philosophy* (Princeton Paperbacks: 1991), pp. xv–xvi.
15. Francis Macdonald Cornford, *Principium Sapientiae: A Study of the Origins of Greek Philosophical Thought*, (Cambridge University Press: 1952) p. 118, p. 189.
16. Cornford, *From Religion to Philosophy*, pp. 75–77.
17. Translation in Walter Willi, "The Orphic Mysteries and the Greek Spirit," *The Meaning of the Eleusinian Mysteries: Papers from the Eranos Yearbooks,* Vol. 2., ed. Joseph Campbell (Princeton University Press: 1979), p. 83. The fragment is preserved in Simplicius' *Commentary on the Physics*, 24. pp. 13–25.
18. Cornford, *From Religion to Philosophy*, pp. 40–41, pp. 62–63, p. 146. See also Cornford, Ch.X, "Anaximander's System," in *Principium Sapientia.*
19. George Thomson, *Aeschylus and Athens* (London: Lawrence and Wishart, 1973), pp. 76–78, p. 147.
20. http://philoctetes.free.fr/parmenides.pdf
21. Thomson, *Aeschylus and Athens,* p. 188.
22. Sohn-Rethel, *IML,* p. 64–71.
23. Sohn-Rethel, *IML,* p. 6.
24. Charles H. Kahn (ed.), *The Art and Thought of Heraclitus: An Edition of the Fragments with Translation and Commentary* (Cambridge University Press: 1981), p. 67.
25. Richard Seaford, *Money and the Early Greek Mind: Homer, Philosophy, Tragedy* (Cambridge University Press: 2004), pp. 310–12.
26. Thomson, *The First Philosophers,* Ch. XIV/5.
27. Luxemburg, "Slavery," *The Rosa Luxemburg Reader,* p. 114.
28. Raya Dunayevskaya, *Rosa Luxemburg, Womens Liberation and Marx's Philosophy of Revolution* (University of Illinois Press: 1991), p. 181.
29. Luxemburg, "Slavery," pp. 111–12.
30. Luxemburg, "The Dissolution of Primitive Communism," *Rosa Luxemburg Reader,* pp. 79–82.
31. Luxemburg, "Slavery," pp. 115–16.
32. Geoffrey Ste. Croix, *Class Struggle in the Ancient Greek World* (Cornell University Press: 1998), p. 40, p. 141.
33. Seaford, *Money and the Early Greek Mind,* pp. 188–89.
34. Cornford, *The Unwritten Philosophy,* p. 248.
35. Seaford, p. 188–89.
36. Seaford, pp. 256–58.
37. Seaford, pp. 247–48.
38. Seaford, pp. 4–11, 102–113, 209–13, 256–58, 292.
39. Seaford, pp. 302–09.
40. Seaford, p. 100, p. 157.
41. Seaford, p. 309.
42. Seaford, pp. 143-44, 259–61.
43. Seaford, pp. 158–60.
44. Seaford, pp. 312–14.
45. Aristotle, *Politics* (Indianapolis: Hacket Publishing, 1998), p. 17.
46. Seaford, pp. 11–12.
47. Seaford, p. 171, pp. 309–10.
48. Walter F. Otto, "The Meaning of the Eleusinian Mysteries," *The Meaning of the Eleusinian Mysteries*, pp. 14–20.

49. Otto, p. 24.
50. Aristotle, Fragment 45, 1483 a 19; quoted in Cornford, *From Religion to Philosophy*, p. 198.
51. Cornford, *From Religion to Philosophy*, pp. 112–13.
52. Seaford, pp. 235–36.
53. Otto, pp. 14–31.
54. Thomson, *Aeschylus and Athens,* pp. 141–54.
55. Seaford, pp. 225–28, p. 263.
56. Seaford, pp. 259–61.
57. Sohn-Rethel, *IML,* p. 203.
58. Hegel, *Lectures on the History of Philosophy, Vol. II.* (London: Kegan Paul 1892), Ch. III/A, Introduction.
59. Brian Calvert, "Slavery in Plato's Republic," *The Classical Quarterly, New Series,* Vol. 37, No. 2 (1987), pp. 367–72
60. Gillian Rose, *Hegel Contra Sociology* (London: Continuum, 2000), pp. 85–86.
61. Hegel, *Lectures on the History of Philosophy, Vol II*, Chapter 3/B/1.
62. Aristotle, *Degen*, Anima.741b21ff.
63. Hegel, *Lectures on the History of Philosophy Vol II*, Chapter3/B/1.
64. Alfredo Ferrarin, *Hegel and Aristotle* (Cambridge University Press: 2001), pp. 115–16.
65. Ferrarin, *Hegel and Aristotle,* p. 315.
66. Hegel, *Philosophy of Mind, Hegel's Encyclopedia of the Philosophical Sciences, Vol. III* (Oxford University Press: 1971), p. 359; Ferrarin, pp. 217–33.
67. Ferrarin, p. 7.
68. Ferrarin, p. 233.
69. Ferrarin, p. 25.
70. Aristotle, *Politics*, III:12.
71. Ferrarin, pp. 96–97.
72. Ferrarin, p. 97.
73. Ferrarin, p. 343.
74. Hegel, *Phenomenology of Spirit*, p. 377. Lukács, *Young Hegel* (London: Merlin, 1977) pp. 480–81.
75. Marx, "On the Jewish Question," *Early Writings* (London: Penguin 1973), pp. 232–33, as translated by Gillian Rose, in *The Broken Middle,* pp. 301–3.
76. Rose, *Broken Middle*, p. 303.
77. Sohn-Rethel, *IML,* p. 57.
78. Sohn-Rethel, *IML,* pp. 111–13.
79. Sohn-Rethel, *IML,* p. 38.
80. Georg Lukács, *History and Class Consciousness* (London: Merlin 1971), pp. 131–33.
81. Sohn-Rethel, *IML,* pp. 125–26.
82. David Hume, *An Inquiry Concerning Human Understanding.* (Oxford: Clarendon Press, 1975), p.165.
83. Sohn-Rethel, *IML,* pp.127–28.
84. Sohn-Rethel, *IML,* p. 75.
85. Sohn-Rethel, *IML,* pp. 13–17, pp. 35–39.
86. Sohn-Rethel, *IML,* p. 74–77.
87. Sohn-Rethel, *IML,* p. 139.
88. Sohn-Rethel, *IML,* p. 36–39.
89. Gillian Rose, *Hegel Contra Sociology*, p. 217.
90. Thomson, *The First Philosophers*, p. 301.
91. Peter Hudis, *Marx's Concept of the Alternative to Capitalism* (Leiden-Boston: Brill, 2012), p. 12. Karl Marx, *Philosophical Manuscripts of 1844, Marx and Engels Collected Works, Vol. III.* (New York: International Publishers, 1975), p. 236, p. 286.
92. Marx, *Capital, Vol. I* (London: Penguin, 1976), p. 132.
93. Sohn-Rethel, *IML*, p. 6.
94. Marx, *Capital, Vol. I*, p. 151.

95. Marx, *Capital Vol. I*, p. 152. Marx refers to Aristotle's *Nicomachean Ethics*, Bk 5 Ch. 5, Loeb edition (London: 1929) pp. 287–89.
96. Marx, "Notes on Adolph Wagner" in *Karl Marx Texts and Method*, ed. T. Carver (Oxford University Press: 1975).
97. Marx, *Capital, Vol. III* (London: Penguin, 1978), p. 970.
98. Hegel, *Philosophy of Mind*, p.386.
99. Marx, *Capital, Vol. III*, p. 957.
100. Sohn-Rethel, *IML*, p. 83.
101. Sohn-Rethel, *IML*, p. 139.
102. Moishe Postone, *Time, Labor and Social Domination* (Cambridge University Press: 1996), p. 169 and pp. 177–78.
103. Andrew Kliman, "A New Look at the Russian Revision of Marx's Concept of 'Directly Social Labor.'" *News and Letters*, Nov-Dec 2005.
104. Sohn-Rethel, *IML*, p. 169.
105. Sohn-Rethel, *IML*, p. 199.
106. Friedrich Engels, *Anti-Dühring*, Part I, Section III. Quoted in Alfred Sohn-Rethel, "The Historical Materialist Theory of Knowledge," (March, April, May and June) *Marxism Today*, April, 1965.
107. Sohn-Rethel, "The Historical Materialist Theory of Knowledge," *Marxism Today*, April 1965.
108. Rose, *Hegel Contra Sociology*, p. 15.
109. Rose, *Hegel Contra Sociology*, p. 17.
110. Cornford, *The Unwritten Philosophy*, pp. 120–26. Benjamin Farrington, *Science and Politics in the Ancient World* (London: Allen and Unwin, 1965).
111. Lukács, *History and Class Consciousness*, p. 111.
112. Georg Lukács, *The Young Hegel* (London: Merlin Press, 1977), p. 54.
113. Lukács, *Young Hegel*, pp. 45–47.
114. Lukács, *Young Hegel*, p. 313, citing Hegel's *Realphilosophie, Vol II*, p. 251).
115. Hegel, *Lectures on the History of Philosophy, Vol I.* Introduction: A/3/c. I have used Helen Macfarlane's 1850 translation, appended to David Black, *Helen MacFarlane: A Feminist, Revolutionary Journalist and Philosopher in Mid-Nineteenth Century England.* (Lanham, MD: Lexington Books, 2004), pp. 61–62.
116. Sohn-Rethel, *IML*, pp. 14–17.
117. C. J. Arthur, "Review of H. Williams' Hegel. *Heraclitus and Marx's Dialectic*; G. Reuten and M. Williams' *Value-Form and the State*; and T. Smith's *The Logic of Marx's Capital.*" *Hegel Society of Great Britain Bulletin* No. 23/24, 1991.
118. I. I. Rubin, "Abstract Labour and Value in Marx's System," *Capital and Class, No. 5,* Summer 1978.
119. Raya Dunayeskaya, "Notes on Chapter One of Marx's Capital and its Relation to Hegel's *Logic*" (1949), in *The Marxist-Humanist Theory of State-Capitalism* (Chicago: News and Letters Publications, 1992), pp. 89–94.
120. Marx, "The Commodity," (first chapter of the first German edition of *Capital*) in *Value: Studies by Marx;* edited by Albert Dragstedt (London: New Park Publications, 1976), p. 27.
121. Marx, *Capital, Vol. I*, p. 173.
122. Dunayeskaya, *The Marxist-Humanist Theory of State-Capitalism* (Chicago: News and Letters Publications, 1992), p. 94.
123. Peter Hudis, "The Death of the Death of the Subject," *Historical Materialism*, 12:3, 2004, p. 163.
124. Herbert Marcuse, *Hegel's Ontology and the Theory of Historicity* (MIT Press: 1989), p. 68.
125. Russell Rockwell, in "Hegel and Critical Social Theory: New Perspectives from the Marcuse Archives," *The Sociological Quarterly*, 45:1, 2004, pp. 141–160, argues that Marcuse, following his favorable approach to Hegel's "historicity" in 1932, progressively retreated from developing the social implications of the *intrinsic* contradiction constitutive of the absolute, finally (in *Reason and Revolution* in 1941), interpreting Hegel's position as the transcendence of the social by a nonsocial ontology.

126. Marcuse, *Hegel's Ontology,* p. 160.
127. Hegel, *Science of Logic*, p. 823.
128. Dieter Wandschneider, "Nature and Dialectic of Nature in Hegel's Objective Idealism," *Bulletin of the Hegel Society of Great Britain*, No. 39/40, 1999.
129. John W. Burbidge, "Hegel's Hat Trick," *Bulletin of the Hegel Society of Great Britain* No. 39/40, 1999.
130. Vladimir Ilyich Lenin, *Collected Works, Vol. 38* (Moscow: Progress Publishers, 1965), p. 234.
131. Dunayevskaya, *Philosophy and Revolution,* p. 27.
132. Ferrarin, p. 56.
133. Quoted in Dunayevskaya, *Philosophy and Revolution,* p. 29.
134. Ferrarin, pp. 56–57.
135. Hegel, *Phenomenology of Mind*, Miller trans. (Oxford University Press: 1977), p. 51.
136. Ferrarin, p. 223.
137. Hegel, *Philosophy of Mind*, p. 576.
138. Dunayevskaya, *Philosophy and Revolution,* p. 29.
139. Martin Heidegger, *Basic Writings,* London: Routledge, 1978), p. 220.
140. Heidegger, ibid.
141. Ferrarin, p. 56–57.
142. Dunayevskaya, *The Power of Negativity,* eds. Peter Hudis and Kevin B. Anderson (Lanham, MD: Lexington Books, 2002), p. 185.
143. Dunayevskaya, *Power of Negativity,* p. 29.
144. Hegel, *Lectures on the History of Philosophy, Vol. III*, pp. 410–23.
145. Hegel, *Logic* ("Smaller Logic") (Oxford University Press: 1975) p. 63.
146. Hegel, *Science of Logic,* p. 824
147. Rockwell, "Hegel and Critical Social Theory."
148. Hegel, *Philosophy of Mind*, p. 577.
149. Ferrarin, *Hegel and Aristotle,* p. 10–11.
150. Dunayevskaya, *Power of Negativity,* p. 241.
151. Dunayevskaya, *Power of Negativity,* p. 9.
152. Theodor Adorno, *Minima Moralia* (London: New Left Books, 1974), p. 148. Quoted by Seaford in *Money and the Greek Mind*, p. 231.
153. Quoted in Seyla Benhabib's introduction to Herbert Marcuse, *Hegel's Ontology* (Cambridge: MIT Press: 1989), p. xviii.

Chapter Two

Critique of the Situationist Dialectic: Art, Class-Consciousness and Reification

1 – ART

Surrealism and the Crisis of the Object

This chapter charts the history and intellectual development of the Situationist International (1957-1971), its forerunner, the Letterist International (S.I.) (1952–57), and the post-Situationist thought of Guy Debord (1932–1994) and his theoretic/political legacy. If there is a "prehistory" of this movement it begins with the Surrealists; not because the Situationists saw Surrealism as the forerunner to their own movement in an avant-garde genealogy, but because the Situationists saw it as necessary to explain Surrealism's "disappearance" as a revolutionary artistic and social force.

In the words of Walter Benjamin (1892–1940): "Balzac was the first to speak of the ruin of the bourgeoisie. But it was surrealism which first allowed its gaze to roam freely over it."[1] Benjamin, in his 1935 essay, "The Work of Art in the Age of Mechanical Reproduction," analyzes the implications of technologies that "liberated" the "forms of creation" from "Art." In the visual field, for example, the masterpieces of fine art could be churned out *en masse* as mechanically reproduced photographic images. In the modern world, the work of art had suddenly lost its "aura" and artists were faced with what the Surrealist, André Breton (1896–1966), called the "crisis of the object." Surrealism, deeply influenced by Freud's ideas on the interrelation of the conscious and the subconscious, recognized that the "residues of the dream-world" lay scattered amongst the products of bourgeois consumer culture;

and that in the waking process of liberation these objects and images could be utilized for poetic invention. In a concrete unity of subjective and objective experience, Surrealism creatively "deviated" the objects of the world from their accepted roles and properties. Surrealism, in Benjamin's estimation, was an expression of dialectical thought in the organic process of historical awakening:

> Every epoch not only dreams the next, but while dreaming impels it towards wakefulness. It bears its end within itself, and reveals it—as Hegel had already recognized—by a ruse. With the upheaval of the market economy, we begin to recognise the monuments of the bourgeoisie as ruins even before they have crumbled.[2]

In 1933, the journal *Le Surréalisme au Service de la Révolution* published a French translation of parts of Lenin's *Notebooks on Hegel's Science of Logic*, which had been published in Russian and German a few years earlier. André Thirion (1907–2001) wrote in a preface, "The effect produced on each of us by reading these texts has led us to recognize in them the greatest power to shock on all who aspire to disentangle the laws of the evolution of all material and intellectual objects."[3] The journal's founder, André Breton, himself made a study of Hegel's *Aesthetics* in order to trace the historical dialectic in art. In the *Aesthetics* Hegel begins with Symbolic art, in which the object is presented not as what it is but as representing something else: in Egypt the labyrinth of the temple symbolizes the movement of the heavens; the sphinx symbolizes the riddle of life itself in the relation of the human to nature. Hegel sees the highest unity of form and content in Classical art: the statues of the Greek gods show them as liberated from abstraction into beautiful, individual, human form. But in the modern age, looking back at the art of Greek Antiquity and the Christian art of the Renaissance, Hegel writes, "No matter how excellent we find the sculptures of the Greek gods, and how fitting and perfect we consider the representations of God the Father, Christ and Mary—we bow the knee no longer." Hegel sees poetry, the most universal art, as having proved itself capable of representing all of the stages of historical life, and therefore as superior to prose. In Romanticism, the poetic art comes into its own—and also reaches its limit. The true content of Romantic thought is absolute internalization in the form of conscious and free personality: "In this pantheon all the gods are dethroned. The flame of subjectivity has consumed them."[4] In Romanticism, the sensuous, material character of art thus loses its ability to express the ideal content it depends on in order to exist as art. For the romantic, the ideal eventually becomes the object which is revealed to the "inner" self. But since "the spiritual has now retired from the outer mode into itself," the "sensuous externality of form" which it assumes becomes impoverished, with "an insignificant and transient character": "Feeling is now everything. It finds its artistic reflection, not in the world of external things and their forms, but in its own expression."[5]

Anna Balakian, commenting in *Surrealism: The Road to the Absolute* on Hegel's critique of Romanticism, writes, "the romantic draws the object within himself and makes an abstraction of it, while the true modern projects himself into the concrete existence of the object."[6] Marshall Berman, in *All That Is Solid Melts into Air,* highlights Goethe's *Faust* as one of the primary sources of the crisis in romanticism, which led to the growth of modernism of the nineteenth century:

> Faust participates in and helps to create a culture that has opened up a range and depth of human desires and dreams beyond classical and medieval frontiers. At the same time, he is part of a stagnant society that is still encrusted in medieval and feudal social forms; forms like the guild specialization that keeps his ideas locked away. As a bearer of a dynamic culture within a stagnant society, he is torn between inner and outer life.[7]

René Crevel (1900–1935) saw Hegel as an ally of Surrealism in the fight against Romantic attempts to obliterate the world in subjective anguish. Hegel, wrote Crevel, had recognized how the narcissistic individual, in devouring the universe and suppressing its objects, "becomes himself the object, and not only becomes insufficient but destroys himself . . . [and] succumbs before the mirror he questioned... the most mediocre, the most vain, the most superficial of waters."[8] Breton saw in Hegel's aesthetics a brilliant insight into the poetic personality's overcoming, through "objective humor," of romanticism's "servile imitation of nature in its accidental forms." Given the repeated efforts of modern art to escape from "servile imitation" in the movements of Naturalism, through Impressionism, Cubism, Futurism and Dadaism, Hegel's assertions had a "tremendous prophetic value."[9]

Hegel saw that in bourgeois civil society the rule of abstract principles in law and economics had negated the organic unity of life. The unity of subject and object which the art of Greek Antiquity once represented had become impossible for a society in which, according to Hegel, the "lower world" of economic nature (once vested in the "family" or "household") promoted a "bestial contempt for all higher values." All sense of the divine had been tossed into the world of "superstition" and "entertainment,"[10] the temple reduced to "logs and stones" and "the sacred grove to mere timber."[11] What then was left for art? Hegel said that "as regards its highest vocation, art is and remains for us something past. For us it has lost its genuine truth and vitality; it has been displaced into the realm of ideas." Hegel did not doubt that works of art would continue to be produced and that artists would strive for perfection with new imaginative techniques. However, what is aroused in us by art *beyond* immediate enjoyment is "the judgment that submits the content and medium of representation of art to reflective consideration." "For this reason," Hegel argued, "the science of art is a far more important requirement in our own age than it was in earlier times when art simply as art could provide complete satisfaction."[12]

In the 1930s, when the art-and-thought police of the Soviet Union were resuscitating romanticism as "socialist-realism" and perverting dialectical philosophy into a positivist materialism, the radicalism of the Surrealists' theory and practice brought them into conflict with the Communists. In 1935, Breton and Crevel were allied with Trotsky at a time when Stalin was preparing for the first Moscow show trials, and the French Communist Party was sponsoring the Paris International Congress for the Defense of Culture, as part of the new "Popular Front" strategy. When Breton responded to some anti-Surrealist slanders written by the Russian Stalinist, Ilya Ehrenburg, by assaulting him in a Parisian street, the Communist organizers excluded him from the Congress. Crevel, who as a theorist was Breton's most important collaborator, committed suicide to protest the exclusion. Other leading Surrealists, notably Tristan Tzara and Paul Eluard, chose loyalty to the Communist Party over loyalty to Breton.[13]

After 1945, Surrealism as a movement found itself weakened by the disruptions of the War, and prone to further splits and defections. And because of the newly found academic respectability of Surrealism's leading lights—and the commercial commodification of their works—soon artists of a new generation were challenging its avant-garde hegemony. One such was Guy Debord. Looking back from the 1950s, Debord credited the Surrealists for having asserted the "sovereignty of desire and surprise" in their projection of a "new way of life." But he found an "error at the root" in the Surrealist idea of the "infinite richness of the unconscious imagination." The "techniques" born of this idea, he argued, such as automatic writing, had tended towards tedium and occultism:

> In fact, the discovery of the role of the unconscious was a surprise, an innovation, not a law of future surprises and innovations. Freud had also ended up discovering this when he wrote, 'Everything conscious wears out. What is unconscious remains unaltered. But once it is set loose, does it not fall into ruins in its turn?'[14]

Furthermore, Surrealism had mistakenly put itself "au service" of a revolution in Russia which had already been lost. In 1967, Debord said, in the *Society of the Spectacle*, that the defeat of the social revolutions following the First World War had left the Surrealists and the Dadaists "imprisoned in the same artistic field whose decrepitude they had denounced." Whereas "Dadaism had tried to repress art without realising it; Surrealism wanted to realise art without suppressing it." What was necessary, in Debord's view, was to project suppression and realization as "inseparable aspects of a single supersession of art."[15]

In the Beginning Was the Letter

In 1947, Gallimard, a major Paris publishing house, put out a book by the young Romanian exile, Isidore Isou (1925–2007), entitled *Introduction d'une nouvelle poésie et d'une nouvelle musique*. Isou analyzed poetic language as having gone through an "amplification" process in the romantic period, followed by a "chiseling" process under Baudelaire, Rimbaud and Mallarme, until Dada finally destroyed it. For Isou, once the chisel of history had done its work, the truth and beauty of poetic language was no longer to be found in words, but in *letters*, representing figures and sounds. As well as experimenting in sound-poems and paintings made up of letters, Isou's "Letterists" (or "Lettrists") sought to challenge the separation between art and life. In a manifesto for a "Youth Front," Isou hailed the youth of France as a sort of subproletariat: alienated by the uninspiring educational system, excluded from consumerism by low pay or unemployment, and oppressed by the archaic French Penal Code. The first act of the Youth Front was a riotous attack on the brutal staff at an infamous Catholic orphanage, which ended in the arrest and imprisonment of some of the youth. In a similar spirit, in 1950, a group of Letterists led by Michel Mourre, disguised as a Dominican monk, disrupted Easter Mass at Notre Dame Cathedral by reading out a "God is Dead" statement. They were attacked with swords by the Swiss guards and almost lynched by the congregation before the police came to the rescue and arrested them. On the cultural front, venerable Surrealists, regarded by Isou as conformist and bourgeois, found their exhibitions and poetry readings disrupted by Letterists shouting "surrealism is dead!" In the field of poetics, Isou attempted to extend the "chiseling" concept to cinema with his *Traite de bave et d'éternité* (Treatise on Bile and Eternity). As an attack on cinematic language, the film uses innovative techniques much repeated by avant-garde directors in the coming years, with its discrepancy between the soundtrack and the images on the screen, and the projection of the physicality of the celluloid itself, "sculpted" with scratched images and corrosive bleach. Isou's voice on the soundtrack says: "I announce the destruction of the cinema, the first apocalyptic sign of disjunction, of rupture, of this corpulent and bloated organization which calls itself film." Premiered at the Cannes Film Festival in April 1951, *Traite de bave et d' éternité* was booed by nearly everyone in the audience and nearly caused a riot. This was, not least, because Isou hadn't actually completed the film, so that for the last ninety minutes of the two-hour film the audience was subjected to the soundtrack in total darkness. Of course, the notoriety of the event, as a radical gesture, added to Isou's avant-garde status. The film (in its completed form) was awarded the Prix des Spectateurs de l'Avant-Garde, at the behest of Jean Cocteau, and was praised by the young Éric Rohmer in the journal *Cahiers du Cinéma.*

In 1952, Isou recruited two young filmmakers to the ranks of the Letterists: Guy-Ernest Debord (1932–1994) and Gil Wolman (1929–1995). In Debord's film of 1952, *Hurlements en faveur de Sade* (Howlings in favor of de Sade) the fragmented soundtrack is accompanied by a completely blank white screen during spoken dialogues. During the silences the screen remains totally dark, plunging the audience into blackness, in which they remain for the final 24 minutes of the film. The soundtrack consists of Letterist sound-poems, howls, quotations from the French penal code and from movies and literature; and importantly, Guy Debord's first articulation of the future Situationist project:

> The arts of the future can be nothing less than disruptions of situations... A science of situations needs to be created, which will incorporate elements from psychology, statistics, urbanism, and ethics. These elements must be focused on a totally new goal: the conscious creation of situations. [16]

The script for *Hurlements*, published in 1952 in the only issue of the Letterist journal *Ion* that ever appeared, refers to images of conflict that never made it into the finished product: rioters fighting police, imperial armies in British India and French Indo-China and Algeria, and a naval battle in the Russo-Japanese War of 1904–1905. The screenplay thus prefigures the use of war footage and Hollywood representations of war in Debord's later films, such as *Sur le passage de quelques personnes* (1959) and *Critique de la séparation* (1961). In 1952, at the first screening of *Hurlements* in Paris at the Ciné-club du Quartier Latin, those who stayed to complain rather than walk out were bombarded by insults and water-bombs thrown by Letterists from the balcony. Those who felt cheated by the misleading title of the film found themselves, literally, "howling for de Sade." Gil Wolman's film, *Anti-Concept* (1952), which employs a similar device of alternating blackness and whiteness, features a strong performance of his improvised sound-poems based on what he called *"mé gapneums*." Wolman's film was banned by the local prefecture, because, not understanding it, they couldn't be sure it wasn't subversive or indecent. One of the key insights Debord and Wolman took over from Isou, is contained in his statement in *Traite de bave et d'eternite* that,

> The history of cinema is full of corpses with a high market value... Screens are mirrors that petrify the adventurous by returning their own images to them and halting them in their tracks. If one cannot pass through the screen of photography to something deeper then cinema holds no interest for me.

It was the "something deeper" that Debord and Wolman were interested in. It soon occurred to them that Isou's chiseling of poetry down to letters had already reached the dead end Surrealism had found itself in with automatic writing. As Vincent Kaufman puts it in *Guy Debord: Revolution in the Service of Poetry*, Debord and Wolman went further than Isou in the direction of decomposition:

> They attacked the letter itself and the made-up words of onomatopoeic poetry by creating a poetry that was purely sound based, as if it preceded linguistic articulation and the production of phonemes, pure breath in search of articulation... They too expressed the loss of communication and, negatively, through provocation, the need to rediscover it. This was to become the task of Situationism.[17]

Debord and Wolman broke with Isou over the "Chaplin Affair." In 1952, at the Paris premiere of Charlie Chaplin's *Limelight,* Debord and Wolman handed out a statement which ended with the words: "the footlights have melted the make-up of the supposedly brilliant mime. All we can see now is a lugubrious and mercenary old man. Go home Mister Chaplin." As Chaplin had been barred from the United States for suspected "communist" sympathies, the Left was deeply offended by the action. The attack was motivated in part by a statement of support for Chaplin put out by leading Surrealists, but mainly by the fact that Chaplin had accepted a medal from the local Chief of Police.[18] The Chaplin incident was too much for Isou, who first praised it, but then backtracked and denied all responsibility. Debord and Wolman took this as their cue to break with Isou and form a rival Letterist group, which they named the "Letterist International."[19]

Unitary Urbanism, Dérive and Détournement

The members and fellow travelers of the L.I. were young; nearly all of them in their teens or early twenties. These "lost children" (*les enfants perdus*) were of the generation that had grown up during the Nazi occupation (some of their parents had been Jewish deportees, or Maquisards), but had been too young to fight in the resistance (the term "lost children," which Debord would never cease to use in describing Letterist and Situationist practice, had its origin in the French revolutionary wars: it meant groups of soldiers, who went out on important skirmishes, from which they did not return). They felt that French youth had been betrayed by the re-imposition of "traditional" conservatism following the Liberation. The authoritarian penal code was kept intact, as was the Gendarmerie which had in large part collaborated with the Nazi occupiers. French imperialism, now revived, was conscripting youth for its wars in Indo-China and Algeria. They also felt betrayed by the bureaucratic, class-collaborationist French Communist Party, the ineffective and dogmatic Trotskyists, the Existentialists and the recuperated Surrealist avant-garde. The headquarters of the new international was a bar in the Arab quarter of Paris's Left Bank. According to one of the regulars, Elaine Papai (who married Jean-Louis Brau, the Letterist poet):

> The life of the Situationist International cannot be disentangled from Saint-German-des-Prés and the climate that once reigned in that neighborhood. The Letterist International had set up its headquarters at *Moineau's*, a low dive in Rue du Four where the letterists were joined by hitherto unaffiliated young revolutionaries. Drugs, alcohol, and girls (especially underage ones) were part of the folklore of the Letterist International, as revealed in certain slogans of that time which, curiously enough, reappeared on the walls of Paris in May 1968. 'Never Work!' 'Ether is freely available', or 'Let us live!'[20]

Another young woman of the group, the Australian artist, Vali Myers, recalls,

> They were the rootless children from every corner of Europe. Many had no home, no parents, no papers. For the cops, their legal status was 'vagrant'. Which is why they all ended up sooner or later in La Santé [prison]. We lived in the streets, in the cafes, like a pack of mongrel dogs. We had our hierarchy, our own codes. Students and people with jobs were kept out. As for the few tourists who came around to gawk at 'existentialists', it was all right to con them. We always managed to have rough wine and hash from Algeria. We shared everything.[21]

Unlike the rest of the avant-garde, the Letterist International refused to be "answerable" to the court of art criticism and the gaze of the "other," refused to seek fame, and refused to market anything its members produced. The L.I.'s mimeographed journal *Potlatch*, which appeared in twenty issues between June 1954 and November 1957, with an eventual print run of five hundred copies, was always given away free to friends of the group; or mailed to people who expressed an interest, or might be interested (or offended). The L.I.'s theory of "unitary urbanism" was first formulated by the nineteen-year-old Ivan Chtcheglov in a remarkable essay published in *Potlatch*, in 1953, on modern urban life and the "utopian" alternative possibilities:

> Darkness and obscurity are banished by artificial lighting, and the seasons by air conditioning. Night and summer are losing their charm and dawn is disappearing. The urban population think they have escaped from cosmic reality, but there is no corresponding expansion of their dream life. The reason is clear: dreams spring from reality and are realized in it. The latest technological developments would make possible the individual's unbroken contact with cosmic reality while eliminating its disagreeable aspects. Stars and rain can be seen through glass ceilings. The mobile house turns with the sun. Its sliding

> walls enable vegetation to invade life. Mounted on tracks, it can go down to the sea in the morning and return to the forest in the evening... The architecture of tomorrow will be a means of modifying present conceptions of time and space.[22]

Unitary urbanism expressed a vision of city planning based on aesthetic and technological innovations in architecture, but freed from subordination to the needs of corporate developers and the endless expansion of private car ownership. Letterist "Psychogeography" involved "the study of the specific effects of the geographical environment, consciously organized or not, on the emotions and behaviours of individuals." This involved the *dérive*: a "technique for rapidly moving through various environments" and of "transient passage through varied ambiances." Given the ravages of homogenized planning in the urban environments of the twenty-first century, with city centers given over to big business and tourism, functionalist architecture, and streets polluted by the noise and fumes of automobile traffic, it is difficult now to re-imagine the experience of the dérive in the Paris of the early 1950s. Chtcheglov could still write of a future in which city dwellers would reclaim the streets: "We will construct cities for drifting... but with light retouching, one can utilize certain zones which already exist. One can utilize certain persons who already exist."[23]

The basic idea of the dérive technique was that the individuals or groups would "drift" through the city and lose themselves (as "les enfants perdus"); their customary rationales for movement (work, relationships and leisure) would be abandoned in order to "succumb to the enticements of the terrain and the encounters associated with it":

> The element of chance is less important here than one might suspect: from the point of view of the dérive, there is a psychogeographic contour map associated with cities, with their permanent currents, their fixed points, and whirlpools that make entering or leaving certain zones quite difficult. But the dérive, as a whole, comprises both this letting-go and its necessary contradiction: the domination of psychogeographic variants through an understanding and calculation of their possibilities.[24]

Despite the Letterists' disdain for the Surrealists, in psychogeography the Surrealist imagination is utilized and renovated, as is evident from Chtchleglov's tribute to Giorgio de Chirico:

> We know that an object, if not consciously noticed during an initial visit, can, because of its absence during subsequent visits, create an indefinable impression: through a correction of time, *the object's absence becomes a sensible presence...* and the impression given to it by the visitor, can range from serene joy to terror... In de Chirico's painting (the Arcades period) an *empty space* creates *fully saturated time*. It is easy to represent the future that similar archi-

> tectures have in store for us, and what their influence will be on crowds [emphases in original].[25]

The "first phase" of the L.I. lasted until 1954, when Debord moved the headquarters from the nihilist atmosphere of the Rue du Four to another bar, this time on the Rue de la Montagne Sainte-Geneviève. But, for Debord, that early phase of the L.I., in which the bloom of youth, like the old Paris Left Bank, passed by them before it could even be seen as what it truly was, the "golden age" of real struggle and potential; and it is this, rather than any utopian vision of the future, that haunts all of his subsequent work. As Kaufman points out, the first thesis of the *Society of the Spectacle*, written fifteen years later (1967), states that in a world in which "all that was once directly lived has become representation," the "separation from, and disappearance of, life has become perfected." By 1968, when the streets of Paris were once again fought over, the city of the Letterists had disappeared.

Asger Jorn, the Artists and the Founding of the Situationist International

In 1954 the celebrated Danish painter Asger Jorn (1914–1973) became aware of, and made contact with, the L.I. Jorn, who had founded the International Movement for an Imaginative Bauhaus in 1953, shared the L.I.'s hostility to abstract expressionism and socialist realism, and saw the concepts of unitary urbanism and psychogeography as in line with his own critique of functionalist design and architecture.[26] An ally of Jorn's was Constant Nieuwenhuys (known as "Constant"), one of the leading lights in a group of artists known as CoBrA (Copenhagen-Brussels-Amsterdam). In 1948, Constant (1920–2005) had argued in the *Manifesto for the Dutch Experimentalists*:

> A new freedom will be born that will allow mankind to satisfy its desire to create. Through this development the professional artist will lose his privileged position. This explains the resistance of contemporary artists.[27]

Debord's new friendship with Jorn, Constant and other leading figures of the artistic avant-garde convinced him that the time had come for the Letterists to shift their focus from the bars of Paris to developments in the wider cultural field of struggle. In an article published in *Potlatch* in 1957, entitled "One Step Back," Debord argued that the L.I., rather than constitute itself as an "external opposition," needed to "seize hold of modern culture in order to use it for our own ends" and join forces with artists—even painters, whose activities has been generally despised by the Letterists. Although Debord accepted that the L.I. might have to initially settle for a minority position within a new international movement, he thought, "all concrete achievements of this movement will naturally lead to its alignment with the most advanced program":

> We need to gather specialists from very varied fields, know the latest autonomous developments in those fields.... We thus need to run the risk of regression, but we must also offer, as soon as possible, the means to supersede the contradictions of the present phase through a deepening of our general theory and through conducting experiments whose results are indisputable. Although certain artistic activities might be more notoriously mortally wounded than others, we feel that the hanging of a painting in a gallery is a relic as inevitably uninteresting as a book of poetry. Any use of the current framework of intellectual commerce surrenders ground to intellectual confusionism, and this includes us; but on the other hand we can do nothing without taking into account from the outset this ephemeral framework.[28]

Debord cannily added that the L.I. needed an expansion of its "economic base," being well aware of the huge amount of money being made out of avant-garde art by the artists themselves as well as the curators and galley-owners. Debord's potlatch anti-book, *Mémoires*, published in 1959, featured collages produced in collaboration with Jorn, who also financed publication of the work. In July 1957, at a conference in Cosio d'Arroscia, Italy, the S.I. was founded. Those attending were, from France, Guy Debord and Michèle Bernstein of the L.I.; from England, the painter Ralph Rumney; from Denmark, Asger Jorn; and from Italy, Guiseppe Pinot Gallizio, the formulator of "industrial painting," Walter Olmo, experimental musician, and Piero Simondo and Elena Verrone of the International Movement for an Imaginist Bauhaus. Debord argued in his *Report on the Construction of Situations and the Prerequisites for the Organization and Action of the International Situationist Tendency* that "the problems of cultural creation can now be solved only in conjunction with a new advance in world revolution." In order to combat the passive consumption he saw defining spectacular culture, Debord called for the international to organize collectively towards utilizing all of the means of revolutionizing everyday life, "even artistic ones."

> We need to construct new ambiances that will be both the products and the instruments of new forms of behavior. To do this, we must from the beginning make practical use of the everyday processes and cultural forms that now exist, while refusing to acknowledge any inherent value they may claim to have... We should not simply refuse modern culture; we must seize it in order to negate it. No one can claim to be a revolutionary intellectual who does not recognize the cultural revolution we are now facing. . . What ultimately determines whether or not someone is a bourgeois intellectual is neither his social origin nor his knowledge of a culture (such knowledge may be the basis for a critique of that culture or for some creative work within it), but his role in the production of the historically bourgeois forms of culture. Authors of revolu-

> tionary political opinions who find themselves praised by bourgeois literary critics should ask themselves what they've done wrong.[29]

The later judgment of the S.I. that production of works of art was "anti-situationist" should be seen in the context of this founding declaration. Although any genuinely experimental attitude, based on critique and supersession of existing conditions, was usable, production of artistic forms was seen as a dead end, leading at best to recuperation and commodification within the spectacle:

> It must be understood once and for all that something that is only a personal expression within a framework created by others cannot be termed a creation. Creation is not the arrangement of objects and forms, it is the invention of new laws on such arrangement.[30]

Constant, on joining the S.I. in 1957, immediately contested what he saw as the utopian shortcomings of Unitary Urbanism. Constant wanted an *artistic* program:

> Those who scorn the machine and those who glorify it display the same inability to utilize it. Machine work and mass production offer unheard-of possibilities for creation, and those who know how to put these possibilities at the service of an audacious imagination will be the creators of tomorrow. The artist's task is to invent new techniques and to utilize light, sound, movement, and any invention whatsoever that might influence ambience. Without this the integration of art in the construction of the human habitat will remain as chimerical as the proposals of Gilles Ivain [Ivan Chtcheglov].[31]

In response, Debord wrote,

> The propositions of Gilles Ivain are not opposed on any point to the considerations of modern industrial production. They are, on the contrary, constructed on that historical basis. If they are chimerical, they are to the extent that we do not have concrete access today to the technical means... not because these means do not exist or because we are unaware of them. In this sense, I believe in the revolutionary value of such momentarily utopian claims."[32]

Within a few months on the founding of the S.I. in 1957, other groups and individuals from Italy, West Germany and Scandinavia affiliated, thus inaugurating a stormy fifteen-year process of fusions, schisms and expulsions, and an equally stormy spread across the globe of Situationist ideas, which were themselves by no means immune to ideological and cultural "recuperation." Kaufman suggests that it would be a mistake to see the exclusions and resignations of the artists (thirty-two in the first four years) as a breakup of, or split in, the S.I., or as a significant change of direction on Debord's part:

> It was a clarification, a return to a stance that was more coherent, more radical, and certainly closer to that of the defunct Lettrist International... Unitary urbanism survived, but in a politicized form, and developed its critical side, freed of the chimeras, utopias, and models that had characterized it until then.[33]

In the world theorized as the "Society of the Spectacle-Commodity," Debord and Wolman argued (in 1956) that art could no longer be justified as a "superior activity" or as an honorable "activity of compensation." In the new conditions of the culture industry only "extremist innovation" was "historically justified." The "literary and artistic heritage of humanity" could however, still be used for "partisan propaganda" because its artifacts could be deflected or "détourned" from their "intended" purposes. In the history of the cinema, D. W. Griffith's Hollywood blockbuster of 1915, *Birth of a Nation,* represented a "wealth of new contribution" but, as it was so despicably racist, it did not deserve to be shown in its original form. Debord and Wolman suggested however, that it might be possible to "détourne it as a whole, without necessarily even altering the montage, by adding a soundtrack that made a powerful denunciation of the horrors of imperialist war and of the activities of the Ku Klux Klan, which are continuing in the United States even now."[34] In *Birth of a Nation* there is a powerful "moonlight-ride" sequence which portrays the Klan as heroes riding to the rescue of the whites. Thirty years after Debord and Wolman's article, Spike Lee actually did "détourne" the scene in *Malcolm X,* borrowing the images of the sequence, but turning its "intent" around, by showing the Klan from the point of view of the victims of its racist terrorism.

Asger Jorn, in an essay entitled "Détourned Painting," published in the Exhibition Catalogue of the Galerie Rive Gauche, Namur, in May, 1959, wrote,

> Intended for the general public. Reads effortlessly.
> Be modern,
> collectors, museums.
> If you have old paintings,
> do not despair.
> Retain your memories
> but détourn them
> so that they correspond with your era.
> Why reject the old
> if one can modernize it
> with a few strokes of the brush?
> This casts a bit of contemporaneity
> on your old culture.
> Be up to date,
> and distinguished
> at the same time.
> Painting is over.

You might as well finish it off.
Détourn.
Long live painting.

Jorn then added, in a section entitled "Intended for connoisseurs. Requires limited attention."

> The object, reality, or presence takes on value only as an agent of becoming. But it is impossible to establish a future without a past. The future is made through relinquishing or sacrificing the past. He who possesses the past of a phenomenon also possesses the sources of its becoming. Europe will continue to be the source of modern development. Here, the only problem is to know who should have the right to the sacrifices and to the relinquishments of this past, that is, who will inherit the futurist power. I want to rejuvenate European culture. I begin with art. Our past is full of becoming. One needs only to crack open the shells. Détournement is a game born out of the capacity for devalorization. Only he who is able to devalorize can create new values. And only when there is something to devalorize, that is, an already established value, can one engage in devalorization. It is up to us to devalorize or to be devalorized according to our ability to reinvest in our own culture. There remain only two possibilities for us in Europe: to be sacrificed or to sacrifice. It is up to you to choose between the historical monument and the act that merits it.[35]

Although Asger Jorn's membership of the S.I. ended in 1961, when he decided he could not reconcile his working life as an artist with the organizational demands of the International, his financial support for Debord's work continued until his death in 1973. The concept of détournement, in the hands of practitioners throughout the world, was to give rise to numerous innovations, such as the subversive use of comic books and pirate radio, and the defacing of advertisements with additional images and words (not to mention René Viénet's *Can Dialectics Break Bricks?,* an over-dub of a Kung Fu movie directed by Doo Kwang Gee). But détournement was further developed by the Situationists into a more general concept of spontaneous rebellion against the technology of consumption. In 1962, an editorial in the *Situationist International* spoke of "new resistances everywhere," especially in wildcat strikes and the "youth rebellion." Even "vandalism" represented a form of resistance against "machines of consumption" as much as the Luddites' "primitive" resistance against mechanized production in the early-nineteenth century: "It is evident that now, as then, the value does not lie in the destruction itself, but in the insubordination which can eventually transform itself into a positive project, to the point of reconverting the machines in a way that increases people's real power."[36] A statement entitled "The Decline and Fall of the Spectacular Commodity Economy" hailed the looting of shops during the Watts/Los Angeles Rebellion of 1965 as a rebellion by young Black proletarians against "the world of the commodity in which worker-consumers are hierarchically subordinated to commodity-values."[37]

2 – CLASS CONSCIOUSNESS

There where they organize themselves as the very form of society in revolution, the proletarian assemblies are egalitarian, not because all the individuals there would come together with the same degree of historical intelligence, but *because together they have everything to do*, and because together they all have the means to do this. [emphasis in original]
Guy Debord and Gianfranco Sanguinetti[38]

Socialisme ou Barbarie

Debord argued in 1961 that the academic specialists had abandoned the "critical truth" of their disciplines to preserve their ideological function. And as, he believed, "real people" were going to come together to challenge the capitalist order, all "real researches" were "converging toward a totality."[39] These "real researches" could be found in "militant publications like *Socialisme ou Barbarie* in Paris and *Correspondence* in Detroit," both of which had broken with Trotskyist vanguardism. Both groups had published "well-documented articles on workers' continued resistance" to "the whole organization of work" and their depoliticization and disaffection from unions which had become "a mechanism for integrating workers into the society as a supplementary weapon in the economic arsenal of bureaucratized capitalism."[40] *Socialisme ou Barbarie*, published from 1949 to 1965, was founded by Cornelius Castoriadis and Claude Lefort. *Correspondence,* published from 1951 to 1962, was founded by C. L. R. James, Grace Lee Boggs and Raya Dunayevskaya (after a split in 1955 Dunayevskaya founded *News & Letters* with Black auto worker Charles Denby). In 1958, Castoriadis, using the pseudonym, "Pierre Chaulieu," was credited as a contributor to the book, *Facing Reality,* alongside James and Boggs.[41] In 1960 Debord joined *Socialisme ou Barbarie,* while retaining membership of the S.I., and remained a member for one year.[42]

Castoriadis (1922–1997) analyzed the implications for radical politics of developments in post-war capitalism, in which the "crisis" and "immiseration" predicted by orthodox Marxism now appeared to have been forestalled. With full unemployment and an increasingly affluent workforce, Castoriadis saw the remaining contradictions of the system as the "alienation" of the worker from work and the division between management and the managed (significantly Castoriadis did not, as did Marx, conceptualize the division as between mental and manual labor). Since *Socialisme ou Barbarie* believed that workers' councils would be the organs for transition to a socialist society, there was a reassessment of the earlier "council communism" which had appeared during the German Revolution of 1918–1919 and its aftermath. In 1952, the Dutch council communist, Anton Pannekoek (1873–1960), wrote to Castoriadis on the issue of workers' councils and the "revolutionary party": "While you limit the activity of these councils to the organization of work in the factories after the seizure of power by the workers, we consider them equally as being the means by which the workers will conquer this power."[43] Whereas Pannekoek thought that the workers would decide for themselves on the organization of the new society once the power of the workers' councils had been established, Castoriadis had drawn up a veritable blueprint for a new "system" of workers' councils, with elections at the shop-floor level for a government of councils and a central assembly which would oversee a "planning factory" for coordinating and managing the economy at the national level.[44]

Pannekoek argued that for councilists to retain even the concept of a party—even a non-vanguardist party—was a "knotty contradiction." Castoriadis, for his part, did not see the role of the revolutionary organization as constituting itself as an external leadership to the working class. He believed revolutionary organization would be necessary to thwart the efforts of Leninist and Trotskyist parties to "take-over" the autonomous bodies that would be set up by the workers. Castoriadis saw *Socialisme ou Barbarie* as building the revolutionary organization of the "avant-garde" minority of workers and intellectuals, whose role in the short term would be to protect the immediate interests of the workers. Although this organization would have to be "universal, minority, selective and centralized," he believed that it could avoid degeneration into a bureaucracy because it would not repeat the fundamental division of management and managed, which the vanguard parties reflected in their theory and practice. Throughout the 1950s the journal carried reports from workers describing the monotony and alienation they felt in their jobs, frequently expressing the view that they, the workers, could self-manage their workplaces much more efficiently and creatively than the existing managers.[45]

The advent of the Hungarian workers' councils in the Revolution of 1956 was seen by Castoriadis as an epoch-making anti-capitalist development. Mistakenly however, he saw Soviet "bureaucratic state-capitalism," with its highly integrated and centralized bureaucracy, as the "highest" stage of capitalism, and therefore ahead of its Western rivals in the domination of labor by capital—not to mention its ideological hold over workers' organizations in the West. This position implied that successful revolution might be even *more* likely in the West, because of the contested democratic space that still existed in bourgeois democracies. However, the events in Hungary did not develop the revolutionary tendencies of the *French* working class; rather they just eroded the authority and hegemony of the French Communist Party. The vote in the referendum of 1958 for De Gaulle's Fifth Republic—90 percent in favor—shattered Castoriadis' faith in the working class as a revolutionary force and led to a significant shift in *Socialisme ou Barbarie* towards covering struggles against alienation in the "superstructure"—especially in culture and education.[46] But for the moment, the "industrial" work continued. In 1959 the journal *Pouvoir Ouvrier* was founded by *Socialisme ou Barbarie* to propagate the program for workers' self-management based on the theories of Castoriadis, as well as to publish reports from workers on the shop floor. But the "knotty contradiction" of party-and-class identified by Pannekoek soon manifested itself. Claude Lefort (1924–2010) broke from the group in 1958 over what he saw as "a permanent contradiction between the theoretical character of the journal and its propagandistic claims." In Lefort's view, which was shared by Henri Simon (born 1922), Castoriadis' position concealed a "radical fiction" posing as a conception of non-bureaucratic socialism, which in turn concealed both a "communitarian" desire for homogeneity and the inevitability of articulation by a small circle of intellectuals.[47]

Another issue was raised by Raya Dunayevskaya (1910–1987) in 1955. She admired the input of reports by workers in the journal: "Heretofore socialists and other radicals have been content with publishing a paper 'for' workers rather than by them. The fact that some now pose the latter question, and pose it with the seriousness characteristic of the theoretical journal, is a beginning." She added however, that to say, "A workers' paper, yes, but in that case it must come from the workers themselves, and not from us the theoreticians," was an evasion of the task at hand: "theoreticians cannot be bystanders to a paper that mirrors the workers' thoughts and activities as they happen."[48] In 1961, Eugene Gogol of Dunayevskaya's News and Letters Committees attended a *Socialisme ou Barbarie* conference in France as an observer and engaged with Castoriadis in discussion of Marx's 1844 *Philosophic Notebooks*, the first English translation of which had been published in Dunayevskaya's book *Marxism and Freedom* in 1958 as an appendix. Castoriadis argued that Marx's 1844 writings had "no bearing on Marxian thought after Marx because they were not published until 1920," and that their philosophic nature made them irrelevant to the question of alienation in modern production.[49]

After Debord broke from Castoriadis in 1961, the S.I. journal *International Situationist* warned that *Socialisme ou Barbarie* ran the risk of "providing an ideological cover for a harmonization of the present production system in the direction of greater efficiency and profitability without at all having called in question the experience of this production or the necessity of this kind of life."[50] A few issues later (in 1963), the critique continued:

> these groups, rightly opposing the increasingly thorough reification of human labor and its modern corollary, the passive consumption of a leisure activity manipulated by the ruling class, often end up unconsciously harboring a sort of nostalgia for earlier forms of work, for the truly 'human' relationships that were able to flourish in the societies of the past or even during the less developed phases of industrial society. As it happens, this attitude fits in quite well with the system's efforts to obtain a higher yield from existing production by

> doing away with both the waste and the inhumanity that characterize modern industry.[51]

Another trend attacked by Situationists was that of depoliticization disguised as "anti-vanguardism." The group founded by Lefort and Simon, *Information-Correspondence Ouvrière* (I.C.O.) was to be criticized by the Situationists during the May Events of 1968 for refusing to "intervene" in the universities to build coordinating bodies for students and workers independently of the vanguard parties. The I.C.O. militants responded that they did not wish to build a "parallel organization" which, like a vanguard party, might "end up substituting itself for the workers." Workers' councils would only come about through "the transformation of strike committees . . . within the dialectic of struggle," not through "ideology." For the Situationists, to whom all "ideology" was anathema, René Riesel hit back, accusing the I.C.O. of disguising an "informal leadership" that "pretends not to exist," while condemning "in amalgam any other possible organisation and to automatically anathematize any theoretical expression."[52]

In *Socialisme ou Barbarie's* first manifesto of 1949, Castoriadis had insisted that Marxism was "beyond question." But in the course of the 1950s he developed the view that Marxism was the ideology of an earlier, "market" and "production" stage of capitalism, and that in the modern bureaucratic world, Marx's *Capital*, for the most part, was no longer relevant. Castoriadis argued that, with the aid of the state, continual expansion of capitalism could take place unimpeded. In the age of state-capitalism and bureaucracy, a new "ideology" was necessary for the new movement towards a system of workers-self management. By the late 1960s the Situationists were attacking what they saw as Castoriadis' "unmistakable progress towards revolutionary nothingness, his swallowing of every kind of academic fashion and his ending up becoming indistinguishable from any ordinary sociologist."[53] Castoriadis himself concluded that Marxism was a "pseudo-scientific" "obfuscation" of nineteenth-century class struggles, which had themselves "allowed the system to function and survive."[54]

The Critique of Everyday Life and the Hegelian Dialectic

The philosopher Henri Lefebvre (1901–1991) was arguably a much more important influence on Debord than Castoriadis. As a young man Lefebvre was a philosophic ally of the Surrealists, before joining the French Communist Party in 1928. In the early 1930s he published the first French translations of Marx's *Philosophic Manuscripts* of 1844 and, unlike Castoriadis, recognized their importance as a vision of "totality" and as a critique of the alienation and fragmentation in working life under capitalism. Lefebvre also published a lengthy commentary for the French translation of Lenin's *Hegel*

Notebooks (1914–1915), published in 1938. Lefebvre's reinstatement of the Hegelian dialectic as foundational for Marx's critique of capital drew charges of "idealism" from the party hacks, who finally expelled him in 1958. Lefebvre argued in *Critique of Everyday Life* (1961) that everyday life, mired in the new consumerism, had stagnated in comparison with the runaway cumulative production of the 1950s. Furthermore, it seemed that the growing rebellion of youth—as represented by the cultural avant-garde—against the impoverishment of everyday life was becoming a more subversive force than the Stalinist-led French labor movement.[55] Debord said in 1961 at Lefebvre's Group for Research on Everyday Life:

> The critique and perpetual re-creation of the totality of everyday life, before being carried out naturally by all people, must be undertaken in the present conditions of oppression in order to destroy these conditions. An avant-garde cultural movement, even one with revolutionary sympathies, cannot accomplish this. Neither can a revolutionary party on the traditional model, even if it accords a large place to criticism of culture... The revolutionary transformation... will mark the end of all unilateral artistic expression stocked in the form of commodities, and at the same time the end of all specialized politics.[56]

It may well have been through discussions with Lefebvre on "totality" that Debord began to engage with the Hegelian dialectic. Anselm Jappe, in his book, *Guy Debord,* argues that, "Debord's theory is *in essence the continuation of the work of Marx and Hegel* and that its importance inheres for the most part precisely in this fact" [emphasis in the original]. Jappe adds in a footnote, "I suspect that I delved too little into Debord's debt to Karl Korsch."[57]

According to Korsch (1886–1961), in the hands of German social democracy Marx's *Capital* provided a theory of ahistorical laws governing production, separate from politics. To reclaim *Capital* for the revolution, Korsch argued, would mean recognizing how it was informed by Hegel's concept of the world-as-totality. In *Society of the Spectacle* Debord quotes Korsch's judgment that, as a "philosophy of the bourgeois revolution," Hegel's dialectic fell short of expressing the entire process of the totality, because in the end it was "not a philosophy of the revolution but of the restoration."[58] Hegel, the last great philosopher, had never managed to supersede theology, and the limitations of philosophy had been inherited by the Spectacle. Following the line of Feuerbachian Marxism, Debord claims that the Spectacle "does not realize philosophy; it philosophizes reality" and becomes itself the material reconstruction of the "religious illusion," the "fallacious paradise" and "the technical realization of the exile of human powers into a beyond."[59]

In Hegel's attempt to reconcile labor and society in a social totality Korsch saw an affinity with the reformism of social democracy. In 1922, Korsch, under the influence of the Russian and German Revolutions, pointed out that social democracy's emphasis on the question of private versus public property could be interpreted in two ways: firstly, as a juridical problem of distribution solvable through changes in the form of the State; or secondly, as a social problem of production which could only be solved by overthrowing the economic structure of society. Korsch argued that because in the social democratic state bourgeois Law and the bourgeois State will not have been totally superseded, the working class would need to control the whole economy, with workers' councils playing a "constitutional" role during the "first phase" of communism to guard against any tendencies in management practices that might lead to capitalist restoration through a bureaucracy.[60] As Debord saw it, Korsch had been proved right on this point: capitalist restoration, in a bureaucratic state-capitalist form, was precisely what had happened in Russia.

Korsch recognized that Hegel had regarded "revolution in the form of thought as an objective component of the total social process of a real revolution."[61] Hegel, however, in his quest for reconciliation with the results of the French Revolution, had preserved the position of thought as external to economic reality. In Debord's view, this externality "could be masked only by the identification of thought with an earlier project of Spirit, the absolute hero who did what he wanted and wanted what he did, and whose accomplishment coincides with the present."[62] This view of the Hegelian absolute as a Cromwellian or Napoleonic embodiment of the Idea in the birth-time of bourgeois society echoes Korsch's later position. By 1938 Korsch was stressing the "bourgeois," rather than the revolutionary character of Hegel's philosophy. Having broken with Leninism, Korsch dismissed the significance of Lenin's *Hegel Notebooks* when they appeared in the1930s, arguing that "Lenin's appreciation of the 'intelligent idealism' of Hegel" came about because "the whole circle, not only of bourgeois materialist thought but all of bourgeois philosophical thought from Holbach to Hegel, was actually repeated in the Russian-dominated phase of the Marxist movement."[63] If, as Patrick Goode says, Korsh viewed Leninism as "merely an ideological form assumed by the bourgeois revolution in an underdeveloped country," then it was no surprise that Lenin was drawn to Hegel: "Leninism was merely an ideological form assumed by the bourgeois revolution in an underdeveloped country."[64] Although Debord seemed unaware of it, in 1950 Korsch, prefiguring Castoriadis' move away from Marx twenty years later, pronounced the same verdict on Marxism as a whole: "Marxism," dependent on the underdeveloped conditions in Germany, had adhered unconditionally to the political forms of the bourgeois revolution. The full development of capitalism, Korsch argued, had negated the working class as agency of socialist transformation and had therefore also negated its "ideology," the politics of the *Communist Manifesto*.[65]

To trace ideology back to revolutions in the "underdeveloped" world is one thing. To resolve all thinkers in these revolutions into ideology/false consciousness is, however, something else; and the Situationists' 1967 text, *Contribution to Rectifying Public Opinion Concerning Revolution in the Underdeveloped Countries* does precisely that, with a similar dose of economic determinism. Franz Fanon's philosophic thinking on the Algerian and Third World Revolutions is lumped together with "Castro-Guevaraism" and casually dismissed as: "the false consciousness through which the peasantry carries out the immense task of ridding pre-capitalist society of its semi-feudal and colonialist leftovers and acceding to a national dignity previously trampled on by the colonists and retrograde classes."[66] The Situationists ignored, or were in ignorance of, Fanon's dialectical concept of a "national consciousness that is not nationalist," which did *not* assert any pre-colonial notion of "national dignity."[67] Interestingly though, this position contrasted with the S.I.'s previous support (in 1962) for the Congolese Revolution, which was described as a coincidence of poetry and revolution, led by "the poet Lumumba."[68]

For the Situationists, their program to "abolish anything within itself that tends to reproduce the alienation produced by the commodity system," should have involved a new openness to such new subjectivities as Third World and Women's Liberation struggles. But these new subjectivities barely featured in Situationist activity or literature. This lack may stem from the primacy Debord gave to class consciousness over all other consciousnesses in his writings of the 1960s; in which case we need to look further at the theoretic basis of his position: the concept of reification, as appropriated from Georg Lukács' *History and Class Consciousness*.

3 – REIFICATION

The Theory of the Spectacle-Commodity and the Influence of Georg Lukács

Georg Lukács (1885–1971) saw in the reformism of social democracy a retreat from Hegel and Marx to Kant. Before Hegel and the French Revolution, the rationalists had treated objectivity as independent of, and separate from, the thinking subject; and for Kant, the object was knowable only in how it appeared to the subjective mind, not as the thing-in-itself. In Hegel's concept of totality this duality in the process of knowledge is resolved by eliminating the autonomy of both the objects and their concepts. The power of the totality is expressed in Lukács' statement in *History and Class Consciousness* that "the chapter in Marx's *Capital* dealing with the fetish character of the commodity contains within itself the whole of historical materialism."[69] In *Capital* Marx shows how the value-form which labor assumes depends on the reduction of the concrete labor to abstract labor, which takes place in the production of commodities through the medium of socially necessary labor time. To raise the issue of commodity fetishism as Lukács did in 1923 was to throw a polemical brick through the window of those communist and social democratic intellectuals who, like Engels, Kautsky and Lenin, had *never* discussed the implications of Marx's chapter on "the fetishism of commodities and its secret." The implications of universalized abstract labor were taken up by Walter Benjamin, in his Arcades Project of the1930s. Benjamin thought that Marx's understanding of the representational logic in commodity exchange illuminated the phantasmagoria of Paris of the Second Empire, in which abstract labor power enforced equivalence of the unequal in the world of the flaneurs, inventors of automatons, photographers, prostitutes, and hack writers, "Whereby the sensuous-concrete counts only as a phenomenal form of the abstract-general."[70]

In the *Society of the Spectacle,* Debord argues that the spectacle does not falsify reality merely in an ideological sense, along the lines of the economic base producing false consciousness in the superstructure; nor does the spectacle constitute itself abstractly as a force external to the concrete social activity of individuals. Rather, the spectacle-commodity and reality each transform themselves into their opposites. The spectacle is a real product of that reality, and "real life," in its subjective passivity, absorbs its own objectified falsification. Their reciprocal alienation is the ground and essence of spectacular capitalism, in which the world is turned upside down:

> The spectacle is able to subject human beings to itself because the economy has already totally subjugated them. It is nothing other than the economy developing for itself. It is at once a faithful reflection of the production of things and a distorting objectification of the producers.[71]

Where then, does this leave proletarian class consciousness? Lukács, in his 1923 essay, "Reification and the Consciousness of the Proletariat," argues that work, as a social-metabolic process, is reified and fragmented in a way that makes people incapable of recognizing the world beyond their own particular tasks as being of their own making. People are rendered passive and contemplative, no matter how "busy" they are.[72] Against the fragmenting yet totalizing power of the commodity Lukács dialectically juxtaposes the particular commodity that production is based on: labor-power. Since labor-power cannot be separated from the laborer, then any real self-consciousness on the laborer's part of that relationship can be "ascribed" as revolutionary. Lukács thus postulates a "subject-object identity" constituted by the class that "wakes up" to mass revolutionary consciousness. Lukács however, is well aware of the gap between the "ascribed" revolutionary consciousness and the actually existing reformist/false consciousness. For

Lukács, reification is the "necessary, immediate reality of every person living in capitalist society." It can be overcome only by "constant and constantly renewed efforts to disrupt the reified structure of existence" and by relating the "concretely manifested contradictions" to the totality of development, and thus becoming conscious of the immanent meanings of these contradictions in their totality.[73]

In Debord's development of Lukács' theory on the issue of passive and contemplative nature of everyday life under capitalism, he sees the leisure industry, with its Club Med holidays, mass sports events, television and movies, as much more than mere distraction. In "consumable pseudo-cyclical time" the commodified moments of leisure are explicitly presented as moments in the cyclical return of real life, but all that is really happening is the spectacle reproducing itself at a higher level of intensity: "The moments within cyclical time when members of a community joined together in a luxurious expenditure of life are impossible for a society that lacks both community and luxury."[74] Debord argues that because the spectacle attempts to establish an illusory unity over the fragmentation and separation, any real proletarian subjectivity cannot confine itself to concerns over egalitarian distribution of wealth; it must be total itself. The real social contradiction is between those who are at home in alienation—or at least feel obliged to maintain it—and those who would abolish it. The coming revolution would require a complete break with Leninist vanguardism as well as anarcho-councilism.[75] According to the 1966 pamphlet, *On the Poverty of Student Life*,

> since the struggle between the system and the new proletariat can only be in terms of the totality, the future revolutionary movement must abolish anything within itself that tends to reproduce the alienation produced by the commodity system—the system dominated by the commodity labor. It must be the living critique of that system, the negation embodying all the elements necessary for its supersession. As Lukács correctly showed, revolutionary organization is this necessary mediation between theory and practice, between man and history, between the mass of workers and the proletariat constituted as a class.[76]

As Debord puts it in *Society of the Spectacle,* Lukács claimed that the Bolshevik form of organization "was the long sought mediation between theory and practice, in which proletarians are no longer spectators of the events which happen in their organization, but consciously choose and live these events." The trouble was, "he was actually describing as merits of the Bolshevik Party everything that the Bolshevik Party was not."[77] The Situationist pamphlet *On the Poverty of Student Life* argues that everything would ultimately depend on how the revolutionary movement resolved the question of "the organizational forms." In concrete terms, this meant projecting the "absolute power of workers' councils as prefigured in the proletarian revolutions of this century." This amounts to an attempt to reinvent council communism as a new "absolute"—but in a new form undisturbed by any vanguard party and (contrary to the *old* council communism) unrestricted by the factory gates.[78] In Lukács' view, consciousness does not just reflect the contradictions and antinomies of the economy; in the modern epoch of capitalist reification economic factors are *in* consciousness *un*consciously.[79] Only through an act of conscious will, involving a "violent" rupture with the system's (unconscious) self-regulation, could the "realm of freedom" be made a possibility. Debord concurs with this analysis in counterposing the proletarian "ego" to the "id" of the economy. The task of the proletariat is to become the "class of consciousness."[80]

Situationist Council Communism

The Situationists' grasp of the difference between class consciousness in-itself and in-and-for-itself was at the root of their polemical attacks on the bureaucratic practices in the workers' movement and the fragmented, contemplative ideas of sociologizing intellectuals. Situationist writings seemed to suggest that workers would reach revolutionary conclusions among themselves and that the S.I. saw no responsibility for helping this process along, unless approached by the workers' councils themselves for assistance. In the period preceding the May Events of 1968 in France, the Situationists were approached, but by groups of students.[81] The Situationists and their new allies made use of the same "detonator" effect Debord had deployed in his Letterist youth. At Strasbourg University in 1966 pro-Situationist students got themselves elected to the leadership of the student union (on a program of abolishing it!) and immediately spent a large part of the union budget on printing 10,000 copies of the Situationist tract, *On the Poverty of Student Life*: considered in its economic, political, psychological, sexual, and particularly intellectual aspects, and a modest proposal for its remedy, written by the Tunisian Situationist Mustapha Khayati. To the university authorities, this was a scandal, and the press, looking for agitators to blame, focused on the Situationists. The pamphlet, spread to a number of universities, and was printed in several editions amounting to perhaps 300,000 copies.[82] Debord decided that the time had come to widen the Situationists' circle of acquaintances, which included *Enragé* students from Nanterre University. Debord knew that something was in the air, and exercised his great sense of timing. The publication of the Society of the Spectacle (1967) put an extra charge in the detonator.

On March 22, 1968, students occupied the administration block at Nanterre University, leading to weeks of protests and the closure of the University for two days. The closure spread the protests to the Latin Quarter and the Sorbonne, which was also occupied. In the course of three days in occupation of the Sorbonne, the Situationists sent telegrams to every factory and union they could think of.[83] As confrontations with the Paris police soon developed into large-scale street fighting, on May 11 the unions called for a general strike on the May 13. When, on May 14, workers at the Sud-Aviation plant in Nantes occupied the plant, supporters of the Enragés and the Situationists in Paris formed the Council for Maintaining the Occupations (C.M.D.O.). With its aim to promote autonomous "councilism," the C.D.M.O. organized the printing of large numbers of pamphlets, such as *For the Power of the Workers' Councils*, and posters, many of which were printed by workers at occupied print shops. As Len Bracken puts it, "The Situationists took great pride in the fact that nothing in these tracts glorified, or even mentioned the Situationist International—above all these tracts called for worker autonomy."[84]

In the wake of the May Events, the Situationists admitted a number of new members and autonomous "sections" of the International were re-established in Scandinavia, Italy and the United States. There was also an explosion of "pro-situ" groups, founded all over the world by those who were influenced by Situationist theory and practice, even though their understanding and motives were treated with skepticism and sometimes distrust by the International itself. Although Debord thought that the French revolt, soon to be followed by the "Hot Autumn" of Italy in 1969, heralded "the beginning of a new era,"[85] he had no intention of building a new political party, either on a national or international basis, that would become, like others past and present, yet another "representation" of the real struggle. Debord felt that the Situationists, as *les enfants perdus*, had no further missions to fulfill in the organizational form they had existed in for the previous fourteen years, and nowhere to return to. In 1972, after a final round of resignations and expulsions, which left Debord and the Italian, Gianfranco Sanguinetti, as the only two remaining members, the S.I. was dissolved at Debord's behest.

The Integrated Spectacle and Globalization

Twenty years after the May Events of 1968, in his 1988 *Comments on the Society of the Spectacle*, Debord identified the dilemma facing the Left well before the fall of the Berlin Wall and the apparent victory of neoliberalism and Thatcher's "There Is No Alternative" (TINA):

> The coherence of the society of the spectacle proves revolutionaries right, since it has become clear that one cannot reform the poorest detail without taking the whole thing apart. But, at the same time, this coherence has suppressed every organized revolutionary tendency by suppressing the social terrains where they had more or less expressed themselves: from trade unions to newspapers, towns to books. In the same movement, one has highlighted the incompetence and thoughtlessness of which this tendency was quite naturally the bearer.[86]

In 1967, building on Lukács' statement about the fate of the worker becoming the fate of the whole of society, Debord had noted the ever-increasing size of the working class and the impending proletarianization of the entire workforce. But in the *Comments* of 1988, Debord, as Jappe puts it, "reversed the terms of this proposition": the conditions of the middle classes *had* become proletarianized in their separation and lack of power but, as they lacked class consciousness, they had negated the power of the proletariat as a force irreconcilable with capital, by absorbing it. In late-Debord thought, the early-Lukács' formulation of a structure of reified consciousness evolves into that of the "integrated spectacle."

Debord's "pessimistic" *Comments* of 1988 should be seen in relation to his original theorizing of the spectacle and the forces resisting it. In the *Society of the Spectacle* Debord, in distancing the Situationists from both the vanguardist and spontaneist positions, said that the revolution "requires" workers to become dialecticians:

> Proletarian revolution depends entirely on the condition that, for the first time, theory as intelligence of human practice be recognized and lived by the masses. It requires workers to become dialecticians and to inscribe their thought into practice. Thus it demands of men without qualification more than the bourgeois revolution demanded of the qualified men which it delegated to carry out its tasks (since the partial ideological consciousness constructed by a part of the bourgeois class was based on the economy, that central part of social life in which this class was already in power). The very development of class society to the stage of spectacular organization of non-life thus leads the revolutionary project to become visibly what it already was essentially.[87]

The idea that the organized working class would become "visibly what it already was essentially" bears a similarity to C. L. R. James' position on the British shop stewards organizations in the 1950s as representing the "future in the present."[88] Debord's reflections about the importance of theory being lived by the masses and the workers becoming "dialecticians" bears more than a passing resemblance to (if not a subtle *détournement* of) Dunayevskaya's portrayal in *Marxism and Freedom* (1958) of Black civil rights activists, women, rank-and-file workers and youth as a movement from practice which was itself a form of theory, demanding the engagement from intellectuals she saw lacking in Castoriadias:

> The task that confronts our age, it appears to this writer, is, first, to recognize that there is a movement from practice—from the actual struggles of the day—to theory; and, second, to work out the method whereby the movement *from theory* can meet it.... Far from being intellectual abdication, this is the beginning of a new stage of cognition. This new stage in the self-liberation of the intellectual from dogmatism can begin only when, as Hegel put it, the intellectual feels the "compulsion of thought to proceed to... concrete truths."[89]

But whereas Dunayevskaya's anti-capitalism became increasingly grounded in philosophy, Debord's did not. In *Society of the Spectacle* Debord quotes Hegel on the "detachment" of "culture" from everyday life that occurs "when the power of unification disappears from the life of man and when opposites lose their living relation and interaction and acquire autonomy." Debord however, does not quote what comes next in the passage: that in the dichotomy between real freedom and bourgeois society "the need for philosophy arises."[90] Dunayevskaya on the other hand, in 1964, contrasts the "subjectivity" of Mao Zedong's elitist voluntarism (which had "no regard for objective conditions") with a "second type of subjectivity" resting on nothing less than the Hegelian "transcendence of the opposition between Notion and Reality" which "absorbs" objectivity: "that is to say, through its struggle for freedom it gets to know and cope with the objectively real."[91] This second subjectivity had two sides: firstly, that the workers were going to rebel whether the theoreticians were interested or not; and secondly, the necessity for theoreticians to stop acting like bystanders and engage with workers' thoughts and activities.[92]

Where did the failure of the mobilizations of students and workers to overthrow capitalism leave Lukács' concept of ascribed class-consciousness? The vagueness of Lukács' statement that commodities would be stripped of the "fetish-character" in a socialist society—he doesn't say how—might give the impression that the "fetishistic forms" are largely a factor of false consciousness, which can be dissolved in the "dialectical conception of totality" and "revealed" as "necessary" illusions once the capitalist state is overthrown and private property and market are abolished or suppressed.[93] In any case, how could "consciousness" in a fully developed capitalist society play the role assigned to it by Lukács—or Debord—whether the agency of revolution be assigned to the vanguard party or the *anti*-vanguard party, based on the spontaneity of the masses? Jappe, who sublates the formulation of the integrated spectacle into Moishe Postone's theory of capital-logic, sees previous theorists as having failed to see that the real "subject" is not the proletariat but capital:

> the secret historic mission of the proletarian movement was to destroy remnants of pre-capitalism, to generalize abstract forms such as those of the law, money, value and commodities, and thus to impose the pure logic of capital… despite the resistance of the bourgeoisie itself.[94]

Jappe is well aware that the accumulation of Capital is dependent on the exploitation of labor power. The worker, as possessor of labor-power must be harnessed to the tools of ever-sophisticated technologies. As a result, capitalists must compete with each other to adopt the latest technologies, and the "strong" must drive out the "weak." In the totality of production the proportion of human labor in relation to the technology decreases, but as human labor is the only source of surplus value, and therefore of profit, the development of technology reduces the total profit of the system. As Jappe puts it, writing in 2011 on the economic crisis,

> Paradoxically, it was the increase in productivity derived from the use of microelectronics that plunged capitalism into crisis. In order to make the labor of the few remaining workers conform to the standards of productivity of the world market, ever more gigantic investments were necessary. The real accumulation of capital threatened to come to a halt. This was the moment when "fictitious capital," as Marx called it, came to the fore. The suspension of the dollar's convertibility to gold in 1971 eliminated the last fail-safe, the last connection between finance and real accumulation. Credit is nothing but an anticipation of expected future profits... Now this crutch is broken, too. The return to Keynesianism, however, which has been suggested to some degree from all sides, will be utterly impossible: there is no longer enough "real" money in the hands of the States. [95]

As Jappe argues, financialization, far from having ruined the "real" economy has helped it to survive past its "expiration date." The role of the system's "gravediggers" is not however assigned to the proletariat. According to Postone, the "real abstraction" of labor reaches the point where the proletariat can only represent "capital-constituting, rather than capital-transcending forms of action and consciousness."[96] Marx, as Postone says, "envisioned a future society as one based on the victory of living labor over dead labor, of the life-world over the system." Postone, however, sees dead labor not as the objectification of living labor alone but as the objectification of historical time that might become the "locus" of emancipation. Abolition of value-producing work would involve bringing back to life the dead labor of capitalist production along with its accumulated knowledge as the historical inheritance of humanity.[97] The former English Situationists, T. J. Clark and Donald Nicholson-Smith, have endorsed the writings of Jappe (and implicitly Postone) as a development of the anti-work ethic of Debord (*abas le travail*).[98] In Situationist thought the "abolition of work" (inasmuch as work is opposed to "life-activity") was inextricably linked with the self-abolition of the proletariat, of which Postone writes,

> For Marx, the proletariat is an object and appendage of capital, one that is and remains the necessary presupposition of capital even as it becomes increasingly anachronistic. The possibility Marx seeks is the self-abolition of the proletariat; this class is not, and does not become, the Subject of history. [99]

For a modern class to "qualify" as an historical subject it must have economic power of some sort, political representation, intellectual leadership and a "program," "historic mission" or *raison d'etre* (though in truth no class in history has ever achieved power *consciously* in this sense). In the case of the bourgeoisie, the "program" can only amount to being, or aspiring to be, at home in the alienation of capitalism. The working class, on the other hand, has never had a "program" for abolishing value-production, and in that sense can be said to have never been more than a pseudo "historical subject," whose objective role has been to push capitalism into developing more efficient forms of valorization. If, as the young Marx said, the proletariat is nothing if it is not revolutionary, then the revolutionary being of the proletariat can only be constituted by its not being, and it can only fulfill its subjectivity by abolishing itself. In the case of the "subjectivity" of capital, for Jappe (following Sohn-Rethel as well as Postone) the logic of value produces an abstract form of consciousness autonomized from authentic human needs and material contingencies, which, nevertheless, *produces* the *real*.

"Value," in reference to Marx's *Grundrisse* and *Capital*, is characterized by Jappe and Postone as an "automatic subject." In the chapter in *Capital* on "The General Formula of Capital" Marx does write of the *appearance* of capital as "an automatic subject" of value, and as "the dominant subject in the process." This particular chapter however, is a discussion of the process of circulation (M-C-M: money-commodity-more money). Marx makes it clear that the "occult ability" of value to "add value to itself" is dispelled once the analysis shifts to the production process and the internal limits imposed by the relation of abstract to concrete labor.[100] In his 1881 "Notes on Adolphe Wagner," Marx states, "for me neither 'value' nor 'exchange value' are subjects, but *the commodity*."[101] The "real abstraction," despite its invisible power, cannot exist in a vacuum, cut off from the objectively real which it abstracts. The commodity labor-power, measured by time, is the "property" of the laborer, but in the world governed by abstract labor there is no such person as an abstract laborer. Totalizing power is proportionate to disintegration within its absolute negativity. The power of capital is limited by—and *only* limited by—the revolutionary potential of human power as its own end.

NOTES

1. Walter Benjamin, *Charles Baudelaire* (London: Verso, 1976), p. 176.
2. Walter Benjamin, *Illuminations* (London: Fontana, 1970), pp. 219–30.
3. Surrealisme, No. 6, 1933. Quoted in André Breton, *What Is Surrealism? Selected Writings*, edited by Franklin Rosemont (London: Pluto, 1978), p. 94.
4. Quoted and translated from Hegel, *Werke, Vol 13*. pp. 141–42, in Jason Gaiger, "Art as Made and Sensuous: Hegel, Danto and the End of Art." *Bulletin of the Hegel Society,* No. 41/42, 2000. "Selections from Hegel's Lectures on Aesthetics," eds. Bernard Bosanquet and W.M. Bryant, *The Journal of Speculative Philosophy* (London:1886).
5. Quoted and translated from Hegel, *Werke, Vol 13*, pp. 25–26 by J. Gaiger, "Art as Made and Sensuous: Hegel, Danto and the End of Art."

6. Anna Balakian, *Surrealism: The Road to the Absolute* (Chicago University Press: 1987), p. 139.
7. Marshall Berman, *All That Is Solid Melts into Air* (London: Verso, 1982), p. 43.
8. Balakian, *Surrealism*, p. 139.
9. Breton *What Is Surrealism?*, pp. 76-82; Balakian, *Surrealism*, pp. 134–39.
10. Quoted in Georg Lukács, *The Young Hegel*, p. 412.
11. Hegel, *System of Ethical Life*, Hegel: System of Ethical Life and First Philosophy of Spirit (State Univ of New York Press: 1988). www.marxists.org/reference/archive/hegel/help/se.htm
12. Quoted in Gaiger, "Art as Made and Sensuous: Hegel, Danto and the 'End of Art'."
13. Herbert M. Gershman, *The Surrealist Revolution in France* (Ann Arbor: 1974), pp.103–07.
14. Guy Debord, "Report on the Constructions of Situations and the Conditions for Organization and Actions of the Situationist International Tendency," *Situationist International Anthology*, edited by Ken Knabb (Berkeley: Bureau of Public Secrets, 1989), pp. 17–20.
15. Debord, *Society of the Spectacle* (Detroit: Black and Red, 1983), p. 191.
16. Debord, *Guy Debord's Complete Cinematic Works* (San Francisco: Bureau of Public Secrets, 2003). www.bopsecrets.org/S.I./debord.films/howls.htm
17. Vincent Kaufman, *Guy Debord: Revolution in the Service of Poetry* (University of Minnesota Press: 2006), p. 84. On the history of Letterism see also Len Bracken, *Guy Debord: Revolutionary* (Venice, CA: Feral House, 1997).
18. Jean-Michel Mension, *The Tribe* (London: Verso, 2002), p. 115.
19. Greil Marcus, *Lipstick Traces : A Secret History of the Twentieth Century* (Harvard University Press: 1990), pp. 279–82, pp. 346–53.
20. Quoted in Mension, p. 33.
21. Quoted in Mension, p. 24.
22. Ivan Chtcheglov, *Formula for a New Urbanism*, *S.I. Anthology*, p. 1–4.
23. Guy Debord, "Theory of the Dérive," *International Situationist,* No. 2 (1958); first published in *Le Levres Neu* 9, journal of the Belgian "Revolutionary Surrealists," in 1956; *S.I. Anthology*, p. 23, pp. 50–54.
24. Debord, "Theory of the Dérive."
25. Chtcheglov, "Formula for a New Urbanism."
26. Kaufman , *Guy Debord,* pp. 131–32.
27. Constant, "Manifesto," *Reflex*, Amsterdam: 1948. www.cddc.vt.edu/sionline/presitu/manifesto.html
28. Debord, "One Step Back," in *Guy Debord and the Situationist International: Texts and Documents* (Cambridge: MIT Press. 2002), pp. 25–27. Quoted in Kaufman, p. 99.
29. Debord, "Report on the Construction of Situations" (1957), *S.I. Anthology*, pp. 17–25.
30. Debord, "Report on the Construction of Situations."
31. Constant, "On Our Means and Our Perspectives," *International Situationist*, No. 2 (December 1958).
32. Guy Debord, *Correspondence, Vol. 1*, 1957–1960 (Paris: Fayard, 1999) translated from the French and quoted in Kaufman, pp. 137–39.
33. Kaufman, pp. 149–50.
34. Guy Debord, Gil Wolman, "Methods of Détournement," *Potlatch: Information Bulletin of the Letterist International*, No. 27 (Nov. 1956). *IS Anthology*, pp. 8–14.
35. Asger Jorn, "Détourned Painting." Exhibition Catalogue, Rive Gauche Gallery (May 1959). Trans. Thomas Y. Levin. www.cddc.vt.edu/sionline/si/painting.html Asger Jorn, *Situationist International Archive Online.* www.cddc.vt.edu/sionline/si/painting.html
36. "The Bad Days Will End" (editorial), *International Situationist, No. 7 , S.I. Anthology*, p. 82.
37. "The Decline and Fall of the Spectacular Commodity Economy" (editorial), *International Situationist,* No. 10. *S.I. Anthology,* pp. 153–60.
38. Guy Debord and Gianfranco Sanguinetti, *The Veritable Split in the International* (London: BM Chronos, 1985), p. 69.

39. Debord, "Perspectives for Conscious Alterations in Everyday Life," *International Situationist,* No. 6, *S.I. Anthology,* pp. 68–74.
40. "The Bad Days Will End" (editorial), *International Situationist,* No. 7. *S.I. Anthology,* p. 82.
41. C. L. R. James, Grace C. Lee, and Pierre Chaulieu (Cornelius Castoriadis), *Facing Reality: The New Society, Where to Look for It, How to Bring it Closer* (Detroit: Bewick, 1974), pp. 34–39; Cornelius Castoriadis, "C. L. R. James and the Fate of Marxism," in *C. L. R. James, His Intellectual Legacies,* eds. S. R. Cudjoe and W. E. Cain (Massachusetts University Press: 1995), pp. 277–97. After 1958 there was no further contact between Castoriadis and James. According to Cudjoe and Cain, Castoriadis was angered because "James published 'Facing Reality' without fully working out the ideas contained in the pamphlet and without having Castoriadis' final approval to publish his section in the pamphlet." In an interview (*Telos* No. 30, 1976) Claude Lefort, speaking on relations between Castoriadis and *Correspondence,* confuses Dunayevskaya with James' then colaborator, Grace Lee Boggs. Marcel van der Linden, in "Socialisme ou Barbarie" (*Left History,* No. 5.1, 1997) compounds the confusion by interpreting Lefort's account as indicating a "close co-operation which had grown between Castoriadis and Dunayevskaya in the 1950s"—which was not the case at all.
42. Kaufman, p. 171.
43. Pannekoek, Anton. "Discussion sur le probleme du parti révolutionnaire," *Socialisme ou Barbarie,* July-August 1952. www.marxists.org/archive/pannekoe/1953/socialisme-ou-barbarisme.htm
44. Richard Gombin, *The Origins of Modern Leftism* (London: Penguin 1975), p. 98; P. Chaulieu, "Sur le contenu du socialisme," in *Socialisme ou Barbarie* (July-September 1957).
45. Gombin, *Origins of Modern Leftism,* pp. 99–100; P. Chaulieu [Castoriadis], "Discussion sur le probleme du parti révolutionnaire," *Socialisme ou Barbarie* (July-August 1952); P. Chaulieu, "Réponse au camarade Pannekoek," *Socialisme ou Barbarie* (April-June 1954).
46. Arthur Hirsch, *The French Left* (Montreal: Black Rose 1982), pp. 108–31.
47. Claude Lefort, "Interview." *Telos,* No. 30 (1976).
48. Raya Dunayevskaya, "A Response to Castoriadis's *Socialism or Barbarism*" (1955), reprinted in *News and Letters,* Oct–Nov 2007.
49. "Letter from Eugene Gogol," *News and Letters Bulletin,* August 1961.
50. Debord, "Instructions for Taking Up Arms," *International Situationist,* No. 6. *S.I. Anthology,* p. 64.
51. "Ideologies, Classes and the Domination of Nature," editorial, *International Situationist,* No. 8. *S.I. Anthology,* p. 102.
52. "Beginning of an Era" (editorial), *International Situationist,* No. 12. *S.I. Anthology,* pp. 225–65; Gombin, *Origins of Modern Leftism,* pp. 112–16.
53. "Lire ICO" (editorial), *International Situationist,* No. 11. *S.I. Anthology,* p. 372.
54. Cornelius Castoriadis, "On the History of the Workers Movement," *Telos,* No. 30, 1976.
55. Gombin, *Origins of Modern Leftism,* pp. 59–65.
56. Debord, "Perspectives for Conscious Alterations in Everyday Life," *International Situationist,* No. 6. *S.I. Anthology,* pp. 68–74.
57. Jappe, *Guy Debord,* p. 182.
58. Karl Korsch, Marxism and Philosophy (New York: Monthly Review Press, 1970), p. 19.
59. Debord, *Society of the Spectacle,* p. 76.
60. Korsch, *Marxism and Philosophy,* pp. 129–41.
61. Korsch, *Marxism and Philosophy,* p. 39.
62. Debord, *Society of the Spectacle,* p. 76.
63. "Lenin's Philosophy," appendix to Anton Pannekoek, *Lenin and Philosophy* (London: Merlin, 1975), pp. 120–32 (wrongly attributed to Paul Mattick; corrected in later edition.
64. Patrick Goode, *Karl Korsch: A Study in Western Marxism* (London: Macmillan, 1979) p. 135. Quoted in Kevin B Anderson, *Lenin, Hegel and Western Marxism* (University of Illinois Press: 1995), pp. 175–80.
65. Korsch, "Lenin's Philosophy"; Korsch, "Marxism and Philosophy, and Ten Theses on Marxism Today," *Telos,* No. 26 (1975–1976).

66. M. Khayati, "Contributions Towards Rectifying Public Opinion," *International Situationist,* No. 11. *S.I. Anthology,* pp. 219–22.
67. Franz Fanon, *The Wretched of the Earth* (Grove: New York, 1965), p. 247.
68. "Editorial Notes: Priority Communication" (editorial), *International Situationist,* No. 7, in *Guy Debord and the Situationist International: Texts and Documents,* edited by Tom McDonough (Cambridge: October Books, 2002), pp. 127–35.
69. Lukács, *History and Class Consciousness*, p. 170.
70. Walter Benjamin, *The Arcades Project*, ed. and trans. Howard Eiland and Kevin McLaughlin (Cambridge: Harvard University Press, 1999) X4a,1. Quoted in T. J. Clark, "Should Benjamin have read Marx?" *Boundary,* Vol. 30, No. 1, Spring 2003.
71. Debord, *Society of the Spectacle,* pp. 8–13.
72. Debord, *Society of the Spectacle,* p. 35. Lukács, *History and Class Consciousness,* p. 86.
73. Lukács, *History and Class Consciousness,* p. 103.
74. Debord, *Society of the Spectacle,* pp. 153–54.
75. Jappe , *Guy Debord,* p. 29.
76. M. Khayati, "On the Poverty of Student Life," *S.I. Anthology*, pp. 319-36.
77. Debord, *Society of the Spectacle,* p. 112.
78. Khayati, "On the Poverty of Student Life." *S.I. Anthology*, p. 334.
79. Lukács, *History and Class Consciousness,* p. 57.
80. Debord, *Society of the Spectacle,* p. 53.
81. "Our goals and Methods in the Strasbourg Scandal" (editorial), *International Situationist,* p. 11, *S.I. Anthology,* p. 204–212.
82. Kaufman, p. 181
83. Ralph Rumney, "Interview," *Vague,* No. 22 (London: 1989).
84. Bracken, *Guy Debord,* p. 171.
85. "The Beginning of a New Era" (editorial), *International Situationist,* No. 12; in *S.I. Anthology,* p. 225.
86. Debord, *Comments on the Society of the Spectacle* (London: Verso, 1998), p. 29.
87. Debord, *Society of the Spectacle,* p. 123.
88. James, Lee, and Chaulieu, *Facing Reality,* pp. 34–39.
89. Dunayevskaya, "Marx's Humanism Today," in *Socialist Humanism*, ed. Erich Fromm (New York: Doubleday, 1965). In 1971, Debord's publisher, Gérard Lebovici (Editions Champ Libre) brought out a French translation of Dunayevkaya's book, *Marxism and Freedom*.
90. Hegel, *The Difference between Fichte's and Schelling's System of Philosophy.* www.homepages.ucl.ac.uk/~uctymjm/teaching/Hegel.htm; Debord, *Society of the Spectacle,* p. 9.
91. Dunayevskaya, *Marxism and Freedom*, p. 157.
92. Dunayevskaya, *Marxism and Freedom,* p. 144.
93. Lukács, *History and Class Consciousness,* p. 13.
94. Jappe, *Guy Debord*, pp. 37–38.
95. Anselm Jappe, "Who Is to Blame" (2011). http://libcom.org/library/who-blame-anselm-jappe
96. Moishe Postone, *Time, Labor and Social Domination* (Cambridge University Press: 1996), p. 371.
97. Postone, pp. 255–56 and p. 356.
98. T. J. Clark, preface to Jappe, *Guy Debord*, p. vii–x. T.J. Clark and Donald Nicholson-Smith, "Why Art Can't Kill the Situationist International," October No. 79, Winter 1997. http://www.notbored.org/why-art.html
99. Postone, p. 276, fn. 42.
100. Marx, *Capital, Vol. I* p. 255. Hudis, "The Death of the Death of the Subject," pp. 161–62.
101. Karl Marx, "Notes on Adoph Wagner," *Marx and Engels Collected Works, Vol. 22* (New York: International Publishers 1989), pp. 533–37.

Chapter Three

Essays 2004–2013

1 – LABOR AND VALUE: FROM THE GREEK POLIS TO GLOBALIZED STATE-CAPITALISM

Alisdair MacIntyre in *Whose Justice? Which Rationality?* says that whereas the Idea of the Good, as represented in Plato's *Republic,* was irreconcilable with the realm of the Greek polis, the concept of *telos* in Aristotle's philosophy was implicitly embodied and acknowledged within the actual social practices of his time:

> Aristotle understood that movement from human potential to its actualization within the *polis* as exemplifying the metaphysical and theological character of a perfected universe. His is a universe structured in a hierarchical way—that is why the hierarchical structure of the sciences is appropriate for giving a real account of such a universe—and each level of the hierarchy provides the matter in and through which the forms of the next higher level actualize and perfect themselves. The physical provides the material for biological formation, the biological the material for human formation. Efficient and material causes serve final and formal causes. [1]

In Aristotle's teleology, nature was characterized by "meaning." Development in nature involved not just causality and mechanical motion but also the potentiality for form in the material itself. Nature, within its own order and hierarchy, was always striving towards the "good." Just as form and cosmos struggled to overcome boundlessness and chaos, so Aristotle's polis sought to control the "unlimited desires" of those within its walls and subdue the "untamed nature" of the foreign "barbarians." Aristotle advocated a polis in which principles of "excellence" and "justice" would be upheld and imposed by men educated in the required "virtues." Education was only suitable for those who were "self-sufficient," i.e., able to command the labor of others and live a life free of toil. [2] Although Aristotle advocated that slaves, women, artisans, manual workers, and merchants be excluded from citizenship, he neverthess recognized a meaningful hierarchy within the ranks of the "excluded." As Murray Bookchin points out in his *Ecology of Freedom*, Aristotle took into account the "higher" level of labor, in which the manual and mental are combined. Aristotle rated the "master craftsman" of "practical intelligence," who understood the "why" as well as the "how" of "good works," as superior to the artisan and as more virtuous than those who desired simply to accumulate wealth. [3]

Jose Perez Adan, in *Reformist Anarchism,* examines the influence of Thomas Aquinas' Aristotelianism on anarchist economics. In the Christianized *telos*, Aquinas (1225–1274) considered production and exchange as subservient to ultimate (divine) ends as well as proximate (earthly) ends. In Aquinas' "commutative justice," mercantile exchange of goods was only legitimate in order to make useful and necessary things available for the public good. Like Aristotle, Aquinas saw money as simply the translation of fixed and invariable value into an easy measure of exchange. Usury—generating money out of want without contributing to the creation of value—was considered a sort of ontological disorder, because it implied that value could be created out of money, rather than labor and moral order. In contrast to the political economists of later times, for whom wages were determined a posteriori by the fluctuating whims of the market, the Medieval Scholastics saw wages as representing an "objective value," upheld by the guilds which stabilized prices and ensured the compensation of producers for their toil and costs of replacing the materials used up. [4]

MacIntyre describes an Aristotelian and Calvinist theology in eighteenth century Scotland for which the basic unit of the "good society" was the household of the small-holding farmer—guided from above by definite social, moral and theological principles. Against this tradition, there arose the new "Anglicizing liberalism" represented by David Hume (1711–1796) and Adam Smith (1723–1790), for whom the basic unit of society was the acquisitive individual. The liberals saw land, like everything else, as just another commodity; and saw the continued existence of the Scottish peasantry as an obstacle to economic development. After the Civil Wars and the Jacobite rebellions of the seventeenth and eighteenth centuries, the bourgeoisie wanted no more talk about how "higher" principles should govern the "natural" order of society. The time had come to recognize that society had become a mass of competing passions and needs which could function "naturally" through the market. What was needed was a political and social structure to facilitate trade, protect private property and quell any "lawless" resistance. This structure, Hume claimed, was essentially what had been established by the "Glorious Revolution" led by "Dutch William" in 1688. [5]

The relationship between labor and "value" in political economy was examined even before the Glorious Revolution by William Petty (1623-1687). Petty argued that the magnitude of a product's value depends on the quantity of labor expended in its production:

> If a man can bring to London an ounce of silver out of the earth in Peru in the same time he can produce a bushel of corn, then one ounce is the natural price; now, if by means of new and more easy mines a man can get two ounces of silver as easily as formerly he did one, then corn will be as cheap at ten shillings the bushel, as it was before at five shillings. *Caeteris paribus* [all other things being equal or held constant]. [6]

In the analysis of the mercantile political economist, James Steuart (1712–1780), the intrinsic value of a silver vase is the material substratum given by nature (the mined silver), while its use value is determined by modifications through the labor of the silversmith. But, although Steuart saw labor as what gives the product its use value, he could only see the profit made on "alienation" of the product as determined by supply and demand.[7] In the value theory of Adam Smith (1723–1790), the "natural price" of the commodity is what was sufficient to pay the rent of the land, the wages of the labor, and the profits of the stock employed in raising, preparing, and bringing it to market. In the interpretation of the original "reformist anarchist," William Godwin (1756–1836), the labor theory of value showed the injustice of a system in which those who labored were impoverished by those who did not labor, and yet owned the wealth produced by those who did. Godwin went further than Smith's call to free industry and enterprise from the fetters imposed by old institutions such as church and state. In the Godwinian *telos*, radical political and moral reforms were urgently needed to dismantle the power of "Old Corruption." Godwin advocated these measures as "proximate ends" on the way to the "final destination" of the good life for all in a free society.[8]

Thomas Malthus (1766–1834) led the counter-attack on Godwin's assertion of the claims of political philosophy against political economy. For Malthus, the most serious obstacle to progress and morality was not old institutions but "human nature," which stubbornly refused to accept wage-slavery and destitution as "natural." Malthus predicted that any substantial increase in the population would lead to universal pauperization, and that Poor Law "welfare" would in time consume all public revenue. He supported the protectionist Corn Laws because he saw the prosperous landowners who benefited from them as providing an ideal market (an "effective demand," in Keynesian terms) for the output of industry (landowners, unlike workers, being consumers-par-excellence). David Ricardo (1772–1823), while accepting Malthus' theory of population and "welfare," took the opposite view on the Corn Laws and the empowerment of the landlord class. In early nineteenth century England, the big landowners, having long expropriated the peasantry, had brought in the Corn Laws for their own enrichment through their domination of Parliament. Also, since the rich landowners had loaned the government the money to fight the Napoleonic Wars, a massive "National Debt" had accrued, which required the state to extend indirect taxation on manufactured goods in order to pay the interest owed to the landowners. Ricardo, recognizing the potentially dangerous power of the landowning class, predicted that, as more and more land was cultivated to provide food for the ever-growing industrial population, the cost of production on the least productive farms would set the price-norm for the whole of agriculture. The landlord class would profit more and more from the ever-rising price of food and rent for land; and, having suppressed free-trade, might monopolize the wealth of society to such an extent that the industrial capitalists would find themselves so starved of investment that the economy might wind down into a "stationary state." According to Marx,

> Closely bound up with this scientific merit is the fact that Ricardo exposes and describes the economic contradiction between the classes—as shown by the intrinsic relations—and that consequently political economy perceives, discovers the root of the historical struggle and development.[9]

Marx argues that although the political economy of Ricardo and his predecessors was "scientific" in its "analytical" method—of proceeding from the phenomenal forms of value to their essence (labor)—it had failed to hold the abstracted essence to account for the concrete forms it assumes in the "real" world. Marx criticizes Feuerbach's approach to the history of religion in a similar vein: it is one thing to discover the "earthly kernel of the misty creations of religion" by analysis of its "apotheosized" forms, but something else to develop these forms from the "actual given relations of life"; the former method (Feuerbach's) is "easier," but it is the latter—Marx's method to be developed in *Capital*—that is truly "scientific."[10]

As the exchangeable value of a commodity was in Ricardo's view based on the relative quantity of labor contained in its production process, the value represented by the quantity of labor was separate and independent of exchange relations. But in attempting to determine relative prices *quantitatively*, Ricardo had assumed that there was no fundamental conflict between the *private* labor of the workers and abstracted *social* labor under the rule of capital (although Ricardo argued that wages should never exceed the level necessary to reproduce the "class of laborers," he did acknowledge that "subsistence" had an historical aspect, in that the provisions for reproducing the class of laborers might need to be more generous for succeeding generations). Marx, in investigating the *qualitative* relation in the value-form, challenges Ricardo's assumptions and also criticizes those who drew socialist conclusions from them. The Ricardian socialist, John Gray, imagined that it would be easy to replace money as the "medium" of exchange with "time-chits" representing labor-time: the worker could then "spend" the time-chits on commodities produced by other workers paid in the same way. The problem with this, in Marx's view, is that in commodity production there is *always* a conflict between the private labor of the workers and the social labor imposed by the rule of capital. Marx says that if it is seen as necessary to transform labors and products into exchange-values, this view has come about because "individuals now produce only for society and in society," and because "production is not directly social, is not the 'offspring of association,' which distributes labor internally."[11]

Reformist anarchism, which theorizes a non-exploitative economy with no conflict between private and social labors, sees in Marx's *Capital* an unfortunate "deviation" from the labor theory of value which seems to rule out "co-operative enterprises" in which workers would receive the "full fruits of their labor," with no appropriation of their product by the capitalist "middle-man." In reformist anarchism the labor theory of value becomes the ideological expression of the struggle through the force of association to "rescue the market" from monopolistic intervention rather than the struggle between labor and capital at the point of production (in present-day campaigns to put "Fair Trade" labels on the products of co-operatives or "eco-friendly" companies in the Third World there is a similar underlying assumption of identity between "private" associated labor and the social labor of the world economy; for as these goods compete with cheaper "unfair" products, made according to socially-necessary labor time, the challenge to the law of value is reduced to the subjective "generosity" of the consumers). On the other hand, Marx does share with the reformist anarchists an Aristotelian legacy. According to Joseph Schumpeter (1883–1950),

> Marx's theory of value is the Ricardian view. . . He was under the same delusion as Aristotle, viz, that value, though a factor in the determination of relative prices, is yet different from, and exists independently of, relative prices or exchange relations. The proposition that the value of a commodity is the amount of labor embodied in it can hardly mean anything else.[12]

Schumpeter does recognize that Ricardo's "absolute" values really only functioned as "exchange values or relative prices," whereas for Marx "values" existed independently of exchange values. Schumpeter says that if we could accept Marx's differentiation, much of his theory would become meaningful and tenable. "Of course," he says, "we cannot." But what if we can? Andrew Kliman, who argues that Marx is indeed investigating exchange value as "the mode of expression" and as the "form of appearance" of "a content distinguishable from it," points out that Marx, in his *Notebooks of*

1861–1863, begins to argue for the first time that, since two commodities of differing materiality are qualitatively equal as exchangeable objects, then they must share a common property of substance: a "third thing," which belongs to each commodity as its "intrinsic value." Kliman contends that Marx, in the opening pages of *Capital*, actually aims "to break from the conception of value as a ratio in exchange" rather than offer a theory of exchange ratios based on relative quantities of labor. Value is "an intrinsic property of the commodity itself"; whereas exchange-value is, as Marx says, "the mere form of appearance," not its "proper content." While it is true that the common property of commodities is that they are "useful" (at least in some sense) and are "products of labor," *this* labor, as labor-power, in finding its expression in value, no longer possesses the same characteristics as when it is the creator of use-values. What remains from the commonality of use-values, is only a residue, a mere abstraction. Although, as use-values, different commodities appear as independent of each other, their exchange value is the relative expression of the *abstract social labor time* that is their substance.[13] Marx praises Adam Smith for establishing the abstract universality of wealth-creating activity in which the object is defined not as various concrete labors—such as farming or mining—but labor as past, objectified labor. Marx writes of Smith's insight:

> Now, it might seem that all that had been achieved thereby was to discover the abstract expression for the simplest and most ancient relation in which human beings—in whatever form of society—play the role of producers. This is correct in one respect. Not in another. Indifference towards any specific kind of labor presupposes a very developed totality of real kinds of labor, of which no single one is any longer predominant.... Not only the category, labor, but labor in reality has here become the means of creating wealth in general, and has ceased to be organically linked with particular individuals in any specific form.[14]

Marx identifies the components of value production as *constant capital* and *variable capital*. Constant capital provides the value transferred from used-up means of production (raw materials and depreciation of equipment). Variable capital is what the capitalist spends on wages in order to obtain the labor-power of the living laborer. Living labor adds new value, whereas constant capital transfers old value created by labor in the past. In Ricardian corn-model terms, prices = wages (as total cost of production) + profit. However, competition between capitals leads to uniformity of the rate of exploitation of labor, so that prices tend to equal costs of production plus an *average* profit. Marx says that, given labor-time measured as exchange ratios, the equilibrium of profitability must be undermined if various industries, employing the same amounts of variable capital, have to input different proportions of fixed and circulating constant capital (the "organic composition of capital"). Firms with smaller profit rates will be starved of investment and forced either to adopt different lines of production or go under. But if the enterprises with different organic compositions of capital are owned by the same capitalist, or a like-minded group of capitalists, acting "en bloc, as totality," then what we have to deal with is the "collective capitalist," for whom "the total capital appears as the share capital of all the individual capitalists together."[15]

Value as "self-moving substance" suffers interruptions due to "revolutions in value": technological development causes the destruction of already existing sums of value advanced by individual capitals that cannot meet the changing conditions. Capitalists, who borrow money in "good times" in order to invest in industries with rising productivity and cheapened means of production, may fall into debt when the value of the constant capital they invested in previously is wiped out by this process of devaluation. Marx does not predict that the rate of profit will bring on a *final crisis.* Rather, the Law is constantly overcome by crises, in which the devaluation of the means of production is made manifest, and the counteracting influences operate to some extent in and through the crises. If capitalist production is, as Marx puts it, "the rule of things over man… the inversion of subject into object and vice versa," then the concept of "value, i.e., the past labor that dominates living labor" does, as Kliman claims, take on "a much greater meaning." In the *Critique of the Gotha Program,* Marx conceives of an immediate post-revolutionary change in the first phase of socialism/communism, in which the worker would be paid according to the amount of work she or he does, so that for the "same amount of work… given to society in one form, he receives back in another." The "revolution" would have to overturn the relationships in the factory, in which, as Marx puts it in the *Grundrisse*,

> The association of the workers... is not posited by them but by capital. Their combination is not their being, but rather the being of capital. To the individual worker it appears fortuitous. He relates to his own association with other workers and to his co-operation with them as alien, as to modes of operation of capital.[16]

Any "anti-capitalist" revolution worthy of the name would have to break with the totalizing and all-consuming "logic" of capital from day one of any revolutionary transformation. In "teleological" terms, the first stage of a post-value-producing society—proximate aims—would have to contain the higher goal of breaking down the division between mental and manual labor—the "final" destination.

(First Published in 2004)

2– REIFICATION IN THE TWENTY-FIRST CENTURY: LUKÁCS' DIALECTIC

In 1923 the Hungarian philosopher Georg Lukács (1885–1971) published his most influential work, a collection of essays entitled *History and Class Consciousness: Studies in Marxist Dialectics*. Lukács' "problematic" of a reified "false" consciousness deeply impacted on the philosophers of the twentieth century, especially Adorno, Sartre, Marcuse, Merleau-Ponty, Debord, Edward Said—and maybe even Heidegger. Lukács continues to engage thinkers in various fields, even if most of them see his socialist "solution" as "class-bound" and therefore historically invalidated by the collapse of the Stalinist system he subsequently embraced.

Commodities and Consciousness

In "Reification and the Consciousness of the Proletariat," the most important essay in *History and Class Consciousness*, Lukács says that in a capitalist society, rational human beings live in a reality that appears to them as alien and irrational, even though they themselves have made it. This contradictory, contemplative "activity" is experienced as *immediacy*; the individual's experience of reification lacks the *mediations* which could reveal it in its totality and point the way towards a "solution." In class terms, Lukács argues, the objective reality of social existence is in its immediacy the same for bourgeoisie and proletariat. This condition is, however, correlated by Lukács' observation that *beyond* immediacy the "specific categories of mediation" which can grasp the totality of reified relations are "fundamentally different" for the bourgeoisie and proletariat, due to their respective positions within the same process.[17] Lukács says of the worker: "Inasmuch as he is incapable in practice of raising himself above the role of object his consciousness is the self-consciousness of the commodity." However, by "adding self-consciousness to the commodity structure a new element is introduced"; for "when the worker knows himself as a commodity his knowledge is practical. That is to say, this knowledge brings about an objective structural change in the object of knowledge." With this change the possibility arises that this "commodity," "conscious of itself" at the level of class consciousness, can constitute itself as a "subject-object identity": a Hegelian "knowledge of totality," from the "standpoint of the Proletariat," in which the categories of existence appear in consciousness, *not* as the determining categories of capitalist economics, but as determinants of the Proletariat's own objective existence.[18]

Lukács does not justify this idea empirically. Rather he formulates an "imputed" (or "ascribed") revolutionary consciousness, which he claims can be determined by relating existing consciousness to the totality of social relationships, so that "it becomes possible to infer the thoughts and feelings men would have in a particular situation," if they were able to assess how that situation, and the interests arising from it, "impact on immediate action and on the whole structure of society."[19] For Lukács, this power to "infer" is embodied in the Party.

Lukács' position on consciousness and commodification is based on his interpretation of Marx's analysis of the "Fetishism of the Commodity and its Secret" in the first chapter of the first volume of *Capital.* Lukács says that the essence of the commodity structure is that it takes on "the character of a thing and thus acquires a 'phantom objectivity,' an autonomy that seems so strictly rational and all-embracing as to conceal every trace of its fundamental nature: the relation between people."[20] However, it is here, at the heart of Lukács' analysis that we must ask: is Lukács being "Marxist" enough? For isn't it the case that Marx's dialectical analysis of concealment and appearance suggests that the fetishism does not just, as in the case of the money-form, "conceal" the "relation between people," but actually constitutes the "relations between people" and people and things "as they really are"? In this reading, the reason the "direct social relations between individuals at work" don't appear is because capitalism is, historically and logically, their negation (such relations existed in pre-capitalist societies, and would also exist in a society based on "production by freely associated men"). Although capital organizes co-operation in production, it isolates individuals in their immediacy and forces them to compete with each other through the social "relation between people" that arrives *post festum* as commodity-exchange on a universal basis.

When Marx asks "Whence, then, arises the enigmatical character of the product of labor, so soon as it assumes the form of commodities?" and answers, "clearly from this form itself," this suggests that the reified relations can only be uprooted by the abolition of commodity production.[21] But Lukács does not seem to rule out the production of commodities in a socialist economy; rather he seems to suggest that commodities would be stripped of the "fetish-character," but produced nonetheless. For all his critique of the fetish-character of commodities, at no time does he locate that character in the form itself. Rather, Lukács' "dialectical conception of totality" dissolves the "fetishistic forms" in consciousness and reveals them as ideological, i.e., "necessary" illusions.[22]

Raya Dunayevskaya argues that in Lukács' transformation of Marx's concept of reification "into a universal, affecting all of society equally," the "becoming conscious" is endowed with a "neutrality," and that for all Lukács writes on the proletariat as the sole revolutionary force, "it does not flow either logically or objectively, either historically or dialectically from his original theory." Crucially, she argues:

> Lukács so overstressed "consciousness" of the proletariat that it overshadowed its praxis which was both material force and reason, so that it left room, at one and the same time, for a slip back into the Hegelian idealism of the "identical subject-object" and into substituting the Party that "knows" for the proletariat.

Dunayevskaya however, recognizes Lukács as having "made his greatest contribution to authentic Marxism by making central to his dialectic the interrelationships of the concepts of 'totality' and 'mediation'." [23] In exploring these concepts, in order see what else flows from his original theory, it is necessary to consider Lukács' critique of Kant.

Totality and Mediation

Kant, in refusing to grant the mechanical sciences an absolute knowledge of objective reality, attempts to preserve a self-determined, ethical (and aesthetic) dimension within the subjective realm of freedom. In his *Critique of Pure Reason* Kant proceeds from Sense-Perception and Understanding to the higher level of Reason, in which particulars and universals are unified into the Idea. But the highest philosophic form of the Idea, as represented by Plato's unconditioned infinite, is for Kant beyond the reach of Reason, because no psychological/sensuous intuition/perception of the empirical world can correspond with it. If we apply the categories supplied by reason to the "infinite" we are caught up in antinomies. These antinomies arise in cosmological/theological questions, such as: does the universe have a beginning and an end in space and time, or, is it endless and eternal? Kant points out that neither proposition can ever be tested and proved. Also the problem of antinomies arises in political issues, such as the ultimate "Good" (as represented by Plato's *Republic*), because of the Kantian "chasm" between "is" and "ought," and freedom and necessity.

Lukács sees Kant's *Critique of Pure Reason* as the most precise expression of the antinomies of bourgeois society which need to be overcome. But Kant is an admirer of Rousseau, who argues that the essential will of the human being is to be free and self-determined. In the *Critique of Practical Reason* Kant presents a moral will that, at its highest level, would attain a concrete notion of human "nature," existing in a universal harmony with the notion of Freedom. Kant accepts the scientific idea of nature as the "aggregate of laws" but, as Lukács points out, in Kant's moral philosophy there is a parallel conception drawn from Rousseau's "value concept" of nature, in which modern rational/scientific institutions are seen as reifying and dehumanizing the life of the "People." Kant sees human feelings as sublime when directed towards a moral destiny, which humans are predisposed towards as an incentive for goodness. And because we can conceive of the possibility of living according to moral reason, that very conception can play a regulative role in our behavior, if not a direct, constitutive role in society.

In the *Critique of Judgment* Kant investigates the idea that the totality—in Rousseau's terms, the unity and freedom of the People under the general will—ought to be established, not as a Beyond, but as a Present. At this point Kant introduces the idea of *teleology*: "the idea of collective nature as a system in accordance with the rule of purposes, to which idea all the mechanisms of nature must be subordinated." Hegel points out that Kant is here "returning" to Aristotle's teleological idea that Nature, as a process, adapts itself to end and intelligence, so that in unity, one element can be seen as a moment of another.[24] Kant's moral reasoning, based on the categorical imperative, subsumes the particular under the general, and subsumes the empirical and the concrete under the ideal and the abstract. However, as a hypothesis, Kant postulates an *intellectus archetypus*: a type of intelligence which would be capable of starting with the particular and advancing to the general; or, in other words, constituting a Good that emanates from the "good" nature of humanity rather than from an abstract ideal that appears to be eternally in conflict with the "crooked wood" of "human nature." Hegel comments on Kant's "intellectus archetypus":

> that this "intellectus archetypus" is the true Idea of the understanding, is a thought which does not strike Kant. Strange to say, he certainly has this idea of the intuitive; and he does not know why it should have no truth—except because our understanding is otherwise constituted, namely such that it proceeds from the analytic universal to the particular.[25]

The reverse process of advancing from the particular to the general (universal) is precisely what Lukács aims for with his concept of "imputed" revolutionary consciousness, in which "it becomes possible to infer the thoughts and feelings men would have in a particular situation" if they were able to situate them within the totality of the social structure and the historical process. Lukács agrees with Hegel that, beyond immediacy, fate and purposive activity recognize themselves and each other within mediation, and that consciousness is able to discern its essence in necessity. Lukács comments:

> To go beyond this immediacy can only mean the genesis, the "creation" of the object. But this assumes that the forms of mediation, in and through which it becomes possible to go beyond the immediate existence of objects as they are given, can be shown to be the structural principles and the real tendencies of the objects themselves.[26]

Lukács says that the absence of such mediation can be seen most starkly in bourgeois political economy. Unlike for the bourgeoisie, Lukács argues, "[f]or the proletariat to become aware of the dialectical nature of its existence is a matter of life and death."[27] This is not just a matter of putting food on the table; there is also the barbarity of war caused by capitalist competition.

Lukács repeatedly speaks of the capitalism of his day, which had just had to survive the First World War and the Russian Revolution, as being in its "final crisis," and he draws on the economic theories of Rosa Luxemburg which sought to explain the economic causes of imperialist rivalry and war.

Luxemburg takes issue with Marx's attempt, in the third volume of *Capital*, to demonstrate that capital becomes its own barrier because of the Law of the Tendential Fall in the Rate of Profit. Luxemburg comments that "there is still some time to pass before capitalism collapses because of the falling rate of profit, roughly until the sun burns out."[28] Luxemburg also tackles Marx's schemas on circulation in the second volume of *Capital*, which show how accumulation can take place in a society consisting solely of workers and capitalists, without breaking down due to underconsumption of goods produced. Marx argues that a crisis of underconsumption can be avoided because of the preponderance of "production of the means of production" over "production of the means of consumption." Luxemburg refuses to see this preponderance as a strictly capitalistic "need" to "accumulate for the sake of accumulation" regardless of actual human needs. Luxemburg argues that the workers and capitalists of the industrialized world do not constitute a large enough market to absorb the output of production and so allow the uninterrupted circulation of surplus value. To avoid systemic breakdown, capitalism needs to have an increasing number of "third person" consumers in non-capitalist parts of the world; hence imperialism, hence the barbarism of imperialist rivalry resulting in World War, and hence World Revolution.[29] Like Luxemburg, Lukács sees no future for civilization in the capitalist form that had spawned the horrors of the First World War and the "anarchy" of the post-war economic crisis—an opinion shared by Trotsky, the Council Communists and various other tendencies. Clearly, this opinion was wrong.

Totality as Globalization

Whatever the shortcomings of *History and Class Consciousness*, the importance Lukács places on Kantianism has been vindicated historically. Kant's 1784 essay, *Idea for a Universal History from a Cosmopolitan Point of View*, considers the idea that human freedom and self-determination, "beyond the mechanical ordering of his animal existence," is willed by nature, "independently of [animal] instinct." Kant's radicalism seems to prefigure the *Communist Manifesto* when he says,

> The means employed by nature to bring about the development of all the capacities of men is their antagonism in society… the unsocial sociability, i.e., their propensity to enter into society, bound together with a mutual opposition, which constantly threatens to break up society. [30]

Kant then, like Lukács, is concerned with the moral individual who confronts an unsympathetic empirical world of mechanical laws. Kant says that history becomes a process—"progress"—which binds individuals together in exploitative relationships. But exploitation contradicts Kant's categorical imperative that no individual should treat other individuals as a means to his or her own ends, but should instead treat them as ends in themselves. Kant says that moral wisdom must remain "an unceasing reproach" to "the realm of brute nature," but he concludes that the best we can hope for is a gradual, "infinite progress" from "is" towards "ought." As a final providential gesture towards bourgeois optimism, Kant postulates an eventual "perpetual peace" on a global scale, quite at odds with the perspective of Rosa Luxemburg (though not quite at odds with that of Kautsky and social democracy). Kant bases his postulate on his expectation that, as traffic, trade and industry spread throughout the world, the leading nations would need to collectively manage the available natural and human resources. To achieve this, nation - would have to recognize that the selfish and increasingly destructive behavior of competing trading powers would become self-defeating. Kant doesn't think the crooked wood of humanity could ever be straightened; perpetual peace would not require everybody to live according to the *moral* law, only that *civil* law be extended to international relations—which would of course enhance the possibility of people living by the moral law. Kant foresees the type of international bodies we have over 200 years later, such as the UN, WTO and G20. Kant does not think revolutions can bring about perpetual peace, but he does think that individuals can prepare for this new world by inward moral improvement. Therefore, he is today the moral philosopher par excellence for the "progressive" New Age "ethical consumer," who believes "change comes from within."

Although it is not impossible that members of the G20 will end up waging war on each other, this does not seem likely in the foreseeable future. The priority for the G20 leaders is to agree on international arrangements which will enable them to extract value from the workers and natural resources of the world "in peace." The "peace" does not of course negate the "right" of the strong-and-willing to invade countries whom they regard as lacking "legitimate" "civil societies" and can be portrayed as a "threat" (such a "right" is, incidentally, prohibited by Kant's maxim that "No State Shall by Force Interfere with the Constitution or Government of Another State").

In the opposition, "anti-globalization," camp, the priority of the G20 protestors is to fight their single-issue campaigns. The NGOs, in order to preserve their "activist" credibility, exert ideological leverage ("moral pressure") on political leaders whom they are very careful about keeping their distance from. Gaspar Tamas rightly refers to this as "statism by proxy."[31] Here again, despite the "anti-globalist" ideology, Kantianism re-emerges in the idea of the "infinite progress" towards a "fairer" and "safer" world, in which the self-edifying consumer becomes the agency for the "oughts" of "Make Poverty History" and "Stop Global Warming."

The "final crisis" perspective of Lukács, Luxemburg and others was invalidated during the course of the twentieth century, based as it was on underconsumptionism. Marx's much-misunderstood Law of the Tendency of the Rate of Profit to Fall, on the other hand, has a serious claim to validity, both logically and empirically—as shown in Kliman's recent book *Reclaiming Marx's* Capital*: A Refutation of the Myth of Inconsistency*.

A "Socialism for the 21st Century"?

For Lukács, in 1922, only after a "laborious process," which would include the "seizure of power by the proletariat" and the "organization of the state and the economy on socialist lines," could the "reified form" of objects be sloughed off. In conclusion, Lukács posed two alternatives: either the proletariat would be "given the opportunity to substitute its own positive contents for the emptied and bursting husks" of the fetishistic forms; or, "it might adapt itself ideologically to conform to these, the emptiest and most decadent forms of bourgeois culture."[32]

Whether or not the term "decadent" had any useful meaning then or now (which is doubtful), clearly the "laborious process" had the opposite effect Lukács hoped for, resulting in a tyrannical state-capitalism. Tamas, in his essay, "Telling the Truth about Class," charts the history of the Left as the retreat "from Hegel and Marx to Kant," as well as "the retreat from socialism to egalitarianism, from Marx to Rousseau, the retreat from critical theory to ahistorical moral critique."[33] Tamas highlights for critical attention Edward P. Thompson's masterpiece, *The Making of the English Working Class*. Thompson, covering the period 1780 to 1832, shows how the working class formed and defined itself as morally superior to, and culturally independent of, the bourgeoisie, thus enabling it to form its first national organization—Chartism—in the late-1830s. But Tamas sees Thompson's approach, along with Gramsci's perspective for working class "hegemony," as Rousseauian Marxism: "Whereas Marx and Marxism aim at the abolition of the proletariat, Thompson aims at the apotheosis and triumphant survival of the proletariat." Unlike Rousseau, Marx is the poet of "Faustian demonism," in which capitalism is the "final revelation" that can only be reached by "wading through the muck of estrangement." Marx "does not oppose capitalism ideologically; but Rousseau does. For Marx, it is history; for Rousseau, it is evil."[34] As Marx puts it in the Communist Manifesto:

> Modern middle-class society, which has revolutionized the conditions of property, and called forth such colossal means of production and traffic, resembles the wizard who evoked the powers of darkness, but could neither master them, nor yet get rid of them when they had come at his bidding.[35]

Tamas argues that with the collapse of traditional Lassallean/Rousseauian socialist, (and Stalinist) parties, along with their sect-like social and political cultures, we can now see that their historical role—in which they upstaged the liberal bourgeoisie—was to clear the way for a class-bound capitalism proper, by removing the historical obstacles: feudalism, fascism and eventually, the statist Rousseauian socialism they themselves had created. The collapse of communism can be seen, in one sense, as a revolutionary-democratic upsurge by the peoples of Eastern Europe demanding their freedom. In another sense it can be seen as the result of Western capitalism's attempt to resolve its own problems: by applying pressure to implode the statist economies of the East in order to integrate them into the restructured "New World Order" that is now simply called globalized capitalism. Despite this supposed assault on "state control," the reality is that, in the post-communist world, bourgeois class interests are, as Tamas points out, taken over more and more by the state.

If what remains of party politics is merely the media-run "debate" on how much of "egalitarian" policy is compatible with the "autonomous" and "final" demands of the economy then can a new "socialism for the twenty-first century" go beyond the "traditional" arguments for workers' control and the "planned economy"? Peter Hudis addresses this question in arguing:

> The restructuring of global capital has undermined not only the basis of liberalism but also versions of radicalism that reduced "socialism" to nationalized property and state control of industry. Yet many in the anti-vanguardist, autonomist and anarchist left stop dead at affirming the need for workers' control without considering how value production subordinates the workers' activity to an alien power even when workers have *political* control over some aspects of the labor process. This reluctance to concretely address what is needed to transcend capitalist value production has left the door open for narrow tendencies to step in and offer various false alternatives.[36]

Indeed, if commodified value-production was uprooted, a step Marx thought absolutely necessary to reach the "realm of freedom," then the proletariat would cease to exist. And there is nothing in either the young or old Marx to suggest that he ever saw the political and cultural self-preservation of the proletarian masses within the alienated world of capitalism as serving any other purpose than the proletariat's abolition of itself as a class—although he believed that many decades would have to pass before the subjective and objective developments brought about revolution. If, as Tamas claims, "Class as an economic reality exists and it is as fundamental as ever," then the extinction of past cultural and political forms doesn't necessarily mean that new ones can't emerge which will go deeper than culture or politics; rather it may provide the impetus for such an emergence to take place. A Rousseauian/Lassallean Marxism there was and might still be. But a Rousseauian/Lassallean Marx there never was. The problem of *History and Class Consciousness* addressed by Lukács remains unresolved.

(First published in 2008)

3 – ENDS OF HISTORY AND NEW BEGINNINGS: HEGEL AND THE "DIALECTICS OF PHILOSOPHY AND ORGANIZATION"

In 1989, Francis Fukuyama's thesis on the "End of History" inaugurated a debate about the massive political shift brought about by the collapse of communism, and the adoption of TINA ("there is no alternative") by the reformist Left.[37] Perry Anderson, in his 1992 essay "Ends of History," noted that with the transformations in the global economy, "the distances between a Korean seamstress, Zambian field hand, Lebanese bank clerk, Filipino sailor, Italian secretary, Russian miner, Japanese auto worker, are vastly greater than those that were once bridged in the Second International."[38] The Second International, which today still has a zombie-like existence in social democracy, certainly organized millions of workers, but it was never truly homogenous, and as a real International collapsed at the onset of World War One in the face of national chauvinisms. There is no doubt, however, that in the twenty-first century the organizational void is even more pervasive than in 1992. The only factor "uniting" the non-homogeneous workers of the world is the global crisis they are being enveloped in. What used to be said of socialism could now be said of the neo-liberal vision of globalized capitalism dreamed up in the Thatcher-Reagan era: "It seemed a good idea in theory but it doesn't work in practice." This is not to suggest that there is any likelihood of a "socialist" transformation through statist re-regulation of the economy; nor that mass protest and activism will spontaneously generate socialist revolutions. Now that the "End of History" is complicated by a seemingly permanent economic crisis, a renewed engagement with the Hegelian dialectic—the intellectual source of the controversy—once again becomes necessary.

According to Alexandre Kojève (1902–1968), of whom Fukuyama is a disciple, Hegel saw Napoleon's victory at the Battle of Jena in 1807 as bringing about the "End of History." The citizen soldiers who dealt the fatal blow to the lordship and bondage of feudalism represented the new synthesis of war and industry in a "universal-homogeneous state." Subsequent history, according to Kojève, has simply confirmed the thesis: the failure of the fascist assault in World War Two was the final nemesis of the "anti-Jacobin" wars; Stalin's Soviet Union imitated the universal-homogeneous state of Napoleon; and the coercive rule of the Communist regimes marked a sort of structural adjustment by the post-Jacobin Left to the rise of the European Union and the USA, and (implicitly) the inevitable triumph of global capitalism.[39]

The claim that Hegel's "absolute" includes a notion of the "end of history" seems to have originated with Engels' essay, *Ludwig Feuerbach and the End of German Classical Philosophy* (written post-Marx, in 1886). Engels argues that the "absolute truth" to be discerned in the materialist appropriation of Hegel's dialectic was that philosophy, not history, had come to an end; Hegel's achievement was to have "unconsciously" shown the way to "real positive cognition of the world."[40] But, as Perry Anderson points out, Hegel did not actually use the term, "end of history." Hegel's concept of universal history in fact owes much to Kant, who had ridiculed the Christian dogma of the Last Judgment at the End of Time and put forward his own concept of history as a purposeful, yet never-ending, human progress towards a state of moral good and happiness.[41]

To begin, so to speak, at the end of the beginning, in Hegel's analysis of the downfall of the Greek polis, the development of "particularity" within the self-subsistent whole "is the moment which appeared in the ancient world as an invasion of ethical corruption and as the ultimate cause of that world's downfall."[42] Self-subsistence and particularity were subsequently redefined in the terms of Roman property law as the relations of "persons" and "things." In Hegel's *Phenomenology of Spirit,* "spirit in self-estrangement," originally created under Roman law, is then re-created under feudalism. As "pure culture," this consciousness tries to reform the unreformable lawlessness of feudalism, but ends up having to reform itself (the Reformation). In the Enlightenment the pure culture of everyday life is portrayed by Diderot in *Rameau's Nephew* as the "rending and tearing [of] everything" by a contemptuous wit "conscious of its own distraught and torn condition."[43] In the French Revolution, spirit in self-estrangement consumes itself in the absolute terror of absolute freedom.

Kojève says that the final chapter of the *Phenomenology,* "Absolute Knowledge," shows that "Historical progress, which represents what is truly historical or human in history, is a mediation by knowledge or by comprehending memory." The dialectic of philosophy and history, expressed in "the shape in which time sets forth the sequential existence of its moments," culminates in "a present that realizes a progress in relation to the Past."[44] In the closing paragraph Hegel writes,

> The goal, which is absolute knowledge or spirit knowing itself as spirit, finds its pathway in the recollection of spiritual forms as they are in themselves and as they accomplish the organization of their spiritual kingdom. Their conservation, looked at from the side of their free existence appearing in the form of contingency, is history; looked at from the side of their intellectually comprehended organization, it is the science of the ways in which knowledge appears. Both together, or history comprehended, form at once the recollection and the Golgotha of absolute spirit, the reality, the truth, the certainty of its throne, without which it were lifeless, solitary, and alone.[45]

This "comprehended spirit," which the young Marx sees as "the *anulling* of time,"[46] marks the "transition" spirit makes from the temporal and historical in the *Phenomenology of Spirit* to the pure idea of Being, *logically* prior to its realization in nature, in the *Science of Logic*. As summarized by Kojève:

> The Infinite in question is *Man's* infinite. And hence the "Science" that reveals this infinite-being is a Science of Man in two ways: on the one hand, it is the result of History—that is, a product of man; and on the other, it talks about Man: about *his* temporal or historical becoming (in the *Phenomenology*) and about his eternal being (in the *Logic*). [47]

In Georg Lukács' interpretation of the *Phenomenology* in *The Young Hegel,* the internalizing recollection in absolute knowledge amounts to the "self-annulment of history."[48] According to Lukács, "externalization" is the "central concept" of Hegel's *Phenomenology.* The great achievement of all of the sections of the *Phenomenology* which *precede* "Absolute Knowledge" was to show how "The enlightenment, capitalism and the French Revolution formed the climax of the journey toward the abolition of every sort of natural immediacy and the realization of externalization." Lukács says of the origins of the term externalization (*Ent ä usserung*) in German idealism:

> Philosophically, the term *En tä usserung* was first used, to the best of my knowledge, by Fichte for whom it meant both that the positing of an object implied an externalization or alienation of the subject and that the object was to be thought of as an "externalized" act of reason. [49]

It may be noted that Fichte's formulation actually expresses the thinking of bourgeois political economy and civil society. Lukács, however, appears to believe that Fichte's insight can be corrected by inverting his subjective idealism, i.e., by defining consciousness as objective, sensuous activity and by seeing "objective society" as becoming the real substance "on behalf of the subject." Only by "estranging itself can the subject recognize itself in theory and practice to be identical with substance."[50] Although Lukács thinks "Hegel's approach to history flows in the direction of historical materialism," he sees Hegel as failing to show the history-making spirit ("objective society") emerging as "the actual driving force, the motor of history."[51] Lukács sees the flow towards materialism as blocked by Hegel's idealist comprehension of history as internalizing recollection. The "self-annulment of history" is "nothing other than the supersession of the forms of objective reality so created and their reintegration into the subject."[52]

As Lukács does not wish to see the historical objectivity of this process annulled by a mystified subject whose goal was inherent from the very outset, he argues that alienation can only be overcome through the true "realization" of externalization, i.e., through a change in consciousness by means of revolutionary will acting in accordance with "objective" conditions. Lukács sees externalization and self-estrangment as the process that characterizes human alienation in capitalist modernity. However, according to Gillian Rose,

> This new form of consciousness which denies the whole order, not just part of it, and is perpetually re-formed or inverted, is called "alienated spirit." Thus the idea that Hegel equated 'alienation' with "externalization" in general is fundamentally mistaken. "Alienated spirit" is a specific determination of spirit which does not characterize the modern period.[53]

The problems of alienated labor under capitalism are not those of alienated spirit in pre-capitalist society. In terms of philosophy of history, Marx counterposes to Hegel's dialectic of self-consciousness and consciousness the dialectic of laboring humanity. Hegel was unable to see the commodity fetishism in industrial production which the class struggles of the nineteenth century were to illuminate for Marx. Therefore it is hardly surprising that Hegel conflated modern abstract labor with labor as praxis. But whereas Hegel is accused by Lukács of collapsing his insights on externalization into an idealist reconciliation with bourgeois society, Lukács himself could be accused of the opposite error: of resolving Hegel's insight into his own vulgar materialism, vanguardism, and decades of capitulation to Stalinism.

In the post-modernist view, Hegel's Absolute Knowledge represents a "closed totality" which excludes the oppressed "Other." But, as in Absolute Knowledge, historical contingency and philosophic comprehension are "both together" subjected to the Golgotha and Recollection of absolute spirit, the absolute turns out to be not the "ultimate" reality but a new beginning and point of departure. Hegel's absolute negativity is the ceaseless movement of historical becoming in which, Hegel writes, "The self-knowing Spirit knows not only itself but also the negative of itself, or its limit: to know one's limit is to know how to sacrifice oneself."[54] In the Absolute Idea of the Logic, Nature is portrayed as the "Other" of the Idea, which at the same time represents the Idea's essential freedom in "Life," i.e., the life of the "self-knowing Spirit" in individual self-consciousness. And because it is also social, self-knowing Spirit has an *organizational* dimension. Raya Dunayevskaya points out in that Hegel's final paragraph of the *Phenomenology* the word "organization" occurs twice: firstly, in recollection of the organization of the spiritual forms "as they accomplish the organization of their spiritual kingdom" in contingent history; and secondly, in "the science of the ways in which knowledge appears" as "their intellectually comprehended organization":

> Heretofore the expression "the two together" or both together was taken to mean practice as well as theory. In fact it isn't practice, it is Science as well as

> philosophy, recollection as well as consummation (that) must undergo the Crucifixion and be "born anew".[55]

This suggests that Hegel does not negate practice by formulating the self-annulment of history. Rather, the integrality of thought ("science") with the entire body of philosophical ideas appears to reach beyond the unity of theory and practice to the synthesis of the concept of organization with the organization of thought. On the idea that Hegel's concept of "science" represents a new beginning, rather than the abolition of objectivity, Dunayevskaya speculates, "Marx certainly must have had something like this in mind when he wrote Freiligrath about organization in the historic as well as the ephemeral sense" (in his letter to Ferdinand Freiligrath of February 29, 1860, Marx spoke of the "party" in "the eminent historical sense").[56] Organization in the "ephemeral sense" means forms of organization that have had their time and collapsed, and whose shortcomings and achievements might be usefully studied by those hoping to supersede them. In the "historic" sense, Marx, in 1860, following the demise of the Communist League, thought that the Communist "party" would spring up again "naturally out of the soil of modern society," which explains why in 1874 he could tell the new German socialist party for whose reformist, Lassallean program he had such disdain, that his analysis in *Capital* some years earlier had been "a theoretical victory for our party."[57]

Dunayevskaya, in her 1953 "Letters on Hegel's Absolutes," does not see externalization as reconciliation. She quotes the following passage in the Hegel's final chapter:

> Spirit is the movement of the self which empties (externalizes) itself of self and sinks itself within its own substance, and qua subject, both has gone out of that substance into itself, making its substance an object and a content, and also supersedes this distinction of objectivity and content.[58]

As Hegel puts it the *Philosophy of Spirit*, what is involved here is "finding a world presupposed before us, generating a world as our own creation, and gaining freedom from it and in it."[59] In Dunayevskaya's view, to see the subject as merely estranging itself in "objective society" by abandoning its substance is to distort Hegel's thinking on externalization and to ignore subjective-objective developments in history:

> So socialism too as it "externalizes" itself in parties, and in this case I mean not the vanguard grouping but the Paris Commune, the Soviets and the CIO and so is Hegel talking about history ... "a conscious self mediating process—Spirit externalized and emptied into time."[60]

In the late 1940s, Dunayevskaya, C. L. R. James and Grace Lee Boggs were co-leaders of a group within the U.S. Socialist Workers Party known as the "Johnson-Forest Tendency" (they left the party in 1951 to found the journal, *Correspondence*). In 1948, James made a study of Hegel's Logic, entitled *Notes on Dialectics,* which reflects on the role in revolutionary history of abstract and concrete universals: from the petit-bourgeois "ideality" of democracy in the English Revolution, to the Second International's program calling for common ownership, to Lenin's new universal propounded in *State and Revolution* of the working population "to a man" participating in the administration of the state and the economy. James uses Hegel's argument against Kant to expose the fixed determinations and categories of Trotskyism in its failure to understand the class nature of the USSR. The Johnson-Forest group argued that what made Stalinism in 1939 different to the Second International betrayers of 1914 could only be grasped by grounding the category of state-capitalism in the dialectic of labor and capital, as set out in the categories of Marx's *Capital.* Since Trotsky had failed to develop such an analysis, it was no wonder that all of his predictions for World War Two turned out wrong. Trotsky had predicted that after the War the Russian bureaucracy would attempt to restore bourgeois property forms and that Communist parties elsewhere would prove incapable of overthrowing bourgeois regimes. As it turned out, the Russian bureaucracy kept the state-property relations intact and imposed them in numerous countries occupied by the Red Army in collaboration with Stalinized Communist parties. In the West the Communist parties, in conformity with the "peaceful coexistence" line from Moscow, ruled out any possibility of overthrowing their capitalist classes and saw fit to dampen any revolts that might get beyond their control. Of the French Communist Party, which wielded enormous influence in printed media and education, James writes:

> It is petit-bourgeois in *every* sense. The great negative fact is that this flood of propaganda and agitation rejects the proletarian revolution. One thing it does not do—it never inculcates the self-mobilized revolutionary action of the organized proletariat. The very nature of this flood shows who it is aimed at, *the revolutionary petty-bourgeoisie*. It substitutes "thought," "education," "information," for the *only means* of self-education, action. It is the main ideological source of the stifling of the proletariat. These publications, their organization and publication, still further widen the social milieu for the new petty bourgeoisie of all types to carry on an essentially bourgeois function. [emphases in original][61]

Trotsky's *Transitional Program* of 1938 perceives capitalism as in its "death agony," and the world political situation as "chiefly characterized by a historical crisis of the leadership of the proletariat."[62] For the post-war Trotskyists, this position still held and the perceived crisis of leadership needed to be resolved within the organizational form of the vanguard party. James, opposing this position, argues that the experience of Stalinism had shown that the problem for the movement had become how to *negate* the vanguard party; spontaneous conscious actions by the masses, already well organized in their workplaces, would negate all the abstract universals that previous revolutions had thrown up and create a new society. Later, in the 1950s, James threw out any concept of organized mediation in the world of class struggle. In *Facing Reality* (1958), he and Grace Lee Boggs said of their perspective: "the organization will not seek to propagate it, nor to convince men of it, but to use it so as to more quickly and clearly recognize how it is concretely expressed in the lives and struggles of the people."[63] Believing that socialism was "inherent in the masses," James argued that the only role left for revolutionaries was to tell anyone who didn't know it that this was so.

Dunayevskaya took a different view. In 1955 she founded the News and Letters Committees as an alternative to the vanguard party concept of organization. The decentralized committee-form, in uniting workers and intellectuals, was based on the recognition that the new political forces that arose from below in the 1950s represented a movement from practice which needed unification with the movement from theory. In 1958, the year Dunayevskaya's celebrated book *Marxism and Freedom* was published, she wrote optimistically:

> So rich are the traditions of America, so uninhibited are the American workers by the preconceived notions of leaders, including those from their own labor ranks, that a new Humanism is evolving. They have no Labor Party to "lead" them or mislead them—and they have no awe of intellectuals like the French Existentialists. That does not mean they reject theory. On the contrary. There is a movement from practice to theory that is literally begging for a movement from theory to practice to meet it. When these two finally do meet—and I have no doubt of their meeting—it cannot be anything short of a New Humanism.[64]

During the course of the 1960s the movement from practice to theory did *not* meet the movement from theory to practice—or vice-versa. In 1973 Dunayevskaya moved an amendment to the News and Letters Committees' constitution which counterposed the "integrality of philosophy and organization" to the "party to lead" concept. But by 1987, when Dunayevskaya was beginning work on a book never to be completed, entitled *Dialectics of Philosophy and Organization*, she was concerned that her organization was failing to achieve such integrality. Dunayevskaya now stressed that although the committee-form and the party-to-lead were opposites, they were not absolute opposites. This would suggest that, if they were absolute opposites, then the committees would be locked into a struggle with vanguardism which would make superfluous all other battles of ideas, if not all engagements with the movement from practice that weren't about fighting those trying to "take over." Dunayevskaya posed the question:

> What have the various forms of spontaneity—councils, soviets, committees, associations, communes—achieved? And why when they did come close to power, it wasn't the political organizations that didn't take them over so much, as that they themselves looked to be taken over? [65]

In 1953, when Dunayevskaya was studying Marx, Lenin and Hegel on the "Dialectic of the Party," the veteran council communist Anton Pannekoek (1873–1960) was in correspondence with Cornelius Castoriadis of *Socialisme ou Barbarie* in France and the *Correspondence* group in the U.S. on the question of workers' councils and the increasingly problematical role of the "revolutionary party." At a time when Dunayevskaya was asking "what purpose does a party or a group serve, and what are its tasks?" Pannekoek was arguing for a unity of theory and practice in which the task of the revolutionary organization would be "essentially theoretical: to find and indicate, through study and discussion, the best path of action for the working class." This, Pannekoek added, "should not be intended solely for members of a group or party, but the masses of the working class." In order to help the workers decide what to do in the workers' councils, "they must be enlightened by well-considered advice" by a group (or united group of various revolutionary tendencies) whose "primary task is to go talk to the workers, for example by means of popular tracts that will clarify the ideas of the workers by explaining the important changes in society, and the need for the workers to lead themselves in all their actions, including in future productive labor."[66]

The fact that Pannekoek, a philosophical follower of the crude materialist Joseph Dietzgen, saw nothing of value in Hegel did not prevent him and James from arriving at similar organizational conclusions, at least in the formal sense, about the relationship between revolutionary organization and spontaneity. In 1987 Dunayevskaya came across Pannekoek's 1952 letter again and wrote of it: "It is extremely important to consider it the ground of all other tendencies, be it various anti-Leninist groups like [Paul] Mattick's or even within Marxist-Humanism," who "act as if the absolute opposites are party/spontaneity rather than party/dialectics of thought." The problem she saw with councilist organization theory was that "both party and mass are forms of organization sans philosophy, and we want organization inseparable from philosophy."[67]

The idea that Pannekoek's organizational position should be considered the ground of all other anti-vanguardist tendencies is not invalidated by the historical shift in activism from industrial struggles to the new social movements. Anarcho/autonomist "People Power" activists see the logical alternative to capitalism as, 1) people taking direct control themselves of the resources and decision-making in their communities and workplaces, and 2) federating communities and workplaces for the democratic running of society and the economy for human needs in an eco-friendly manner. The political party is absent from this perspective, except in the Pannekoekian sense of a movement advocating that ends and means be merged into one process. Pannekoek told Castoriadis, concerning workers' councils, "While you restrict the activity of these organisms to the organization of labor in factories after the taking of social power by the workers, we consider them as also being the organisms by means of which the workers will conquer this power."[68]

But history has shown that the problem Dunayevskaya identified remains: the various forms of spontaneity, when they do come close to power, themselves look to be taken over by political organization. In such circumstances the question of "What Happens After" should become paramount. The political heirs of Pannekoek would say that the question of What Happens After is for the workers to decide once the councils are established. But consider Poland and Iran in 1979–1981; in both countries the mass movements seemed to have a tremendous spontaneous creativity with the necessary ingredients for social transformation, including women's movements and workers' councils. And yet both movements were easily taken over, in one case by Catholic reactionaries and in the other by Islamic fundamentalists. In both instances the question of What Happens After was not put forth, even by the radical Left. Marx's description of capital in the *Grundrisse* as "the all-dominating economic power of bourgeois society"[69] shows that if capital remains and relations of labor at the point of production remain unchanged, then political decision-making will necessarily operate within the limits capital imposes. The fetishized form of the commodity is a materialization, not of the producers' subjectivity, but of the objective relations of production; the reification of labor manifests itself in all of the subsequent fetishized forms—including Stalinist state-capitalism and all other false alternatives.

Dunayevskaya, in an outline for *Dialectics of Philosophy and Organization*, said that she couldn't foresee the conclusion and that it would be an "untrodden path" for the organization. But an untrodden path still has to go somewhere. And there is no point in building a hut halfway from which one can only look back from whence one came. The group that broke with *News and Letters* in 2008 to found the International Marxist-Humanist Organization saw the News and Letters Committees as having failed to tackle the task of working out a philosophically grounded alternative to capitalism, preferring instead to simply repeat conclusions and give lip service to the ideas of Dunayevskaya, who herself had stressed that working out the question "what happens after the revolution" before it occurs is crucial for overcoming one of the most important and unresolved problems in the history of Marxism—the separation of philosophy from organization:

> At the point when the theoretic form reaches philosophy, the challenge demands that we synthesize not only the new relations of theory to practice, and all the forces of revolution, but philosophy's "suffering, patience, and labor of the negative," i.e., experiencing absolute negativity.[70]

It is not enough to follow the negative rejections of vanguardism made by Pannekoek, C. L. R. James and Castoriadis, which are defined by what they critique in such a way as to never figure out how to present organizational responsibility for philosophy as the critical mediation. Exercising the power of philosophy in class struggles must involve an organizational form for both eliciting from the masses their own thoughts and for working out a perspective for a new society in which the capitalist value form is overcome.

(2013)

CONCLUSION – PHILOSOPHY AND REVOLUTION IN THE TWENTY-FIRST CENTURY

The Legacy of Postmodernism

The British philosopher Gillian Rose (1947–1995), in her last philosophical work, *Mourning Becomes the Law* (1995), bemoaned the "mixture of naivety and cynicism, without reason and in despair" that she saw in postmodernist thought:

> It is strange to live in a time when philosophy has found so many ways to damage if not destroy itself. One by one all of the classical preoccupations of philosophy have been discredited and discarded: eternity, reason, truth, representation, justice, freedom, beauty and the Good. The dismissal of "metaphysics" is accompanied by the unabated search for a *new ethics*. Yet no one seems to have considered what philosophical resources remain for an ethics when so much of the live tradition is disqualified and deadened.[71]

Postmodernism became predominant at the end of the 1970s as a response from within the Left to disorientation and decline. In the West, following the structural capitalist crisis of the 1970s, the hard-won gains of the working class were rolled back as Fordism was dismantled and the post-World War Two consensus abandoned. As the "postindustrial," "knowledge" economy took off in the West, the enfeebled form of state-capitalism calling itself socialism in the Soviet Bloc and Yugoslavia began to fall apart and give way to warring nationalisms and the "free market." In the Third World, the radicalism of the regimes thrown up by the Anti-Colonial revolutions was undermined from within by corrupt authoritarianism in collaboration with neo-colonialism, and from without by imperialist intervention, which often took the form of "war by proxy" between the super-powers (as in Ethiopia, Afghanistan and elsewhere).

Postmodernist theory, as formulated by Jean-François Lyotard in 1979, called for a final showdown with the "grand narratives" of modernity and the "rhetoric of totality" expressed in Hegel's philosophy of history and in Marx's supposed "universalizing" of the proletariat as the historical agency of socialist emancipation. For Lyotard, the task had become not the completion of modernity, but rather to recognize that it had been liquidated, and that its lack of "reality" had produced "the invention of other realities": hence the association of postmodernism with notions of diversity, multiculturalism and identity politics.[72]

In the postmodern world, according to Rose in 1995, "philosophic 'truth' or 'reason'… are charged with legitimizing forms of domination which have destroyed or dispossessed their 'others' in the name of universal interest." The results of disengagement from the "grand narratives" of philosophic reason could be seen in the upsurge in the 1990s of libertarianism and communitarianism, which, while opposites, are by no means absolute opposites. Homologous to the anti-statism which the libertarians and communitarians shared were the attacks on the welfare state and bureaucratic "socialism." But, as libertarianism presupposes "formal rationality," and communitarianism presupposes "traditional authority," both are types of "legitimizing domination as authority." The commercial and consumer "rights" promoted by libertarianism presuppose the inequalities of capitalist society and the reinforcement of police coercion. Communitarian "empowerment" politics legitimizes the "potential tyranny of the local or particular community," in which it is "the abused who become the abusers."[73] The first years of the twenty-first century have seen how this has played out. The internal contradictions of both libertarianism and communitarianism explain the difficulties of incorporating them into policy-making. This is evident from the efforts of the Conservative British Prime Minister, David Cameron, to promote the communitarian "Big Society" concept at a time of huge cuts in public spending on community projects; and from the previous "Third Way" strategy of Tony Blair's New Labour Party, which combined a roll-back of welfare entitlements with an ill-fated deregulation of finance capital.

For libertarian secularism the struggle against religious fundamentalism has the goal of establishing a civil society based on the formal rationality of right to property and liberty. Libertarians counterpose these perceived "Western" or "Cosmopolitan" values to the "traditional authority" of diverse fundamentalisms. The fundamentalists, sometimes under the banner of "multiculturalism," fight to preserve, or reinstate, the "right" to abuse those who threaten the tyranny of the "community." On the Left, in Britain, the mass protest movement of 2003 against the Iraq War led to the strange communitarian popular front of Leftists and Islamists in a new political party named "Respect," which got George Galloway twice elected as a Member of Parliament. In contrast, the libertarian Left, concerned with rights of women and gays, and the intrusion of religious factions into education and the policy-making bodies of civil society, takes its "formal rationality" from the New Atheism, best represented by the crude materialism of Richard Dawkins.

Hegel was opposed to both the mysticism of religious reaction and the narrow rationalism he discerned in enlightenment liberalism. Hegel's thinking on the history of the Christian religion presupposes the separation of law and custom in the Roman Empire which allowed Roman Law to distinguish between the rights of those who owned property (defined as "persons") and those who had no rights at all, being non-citizens, or those who were someone else's personal property (defined as "things"). The religion of the Roman state, as Gillian Rose explains, actively represents the gods to the people in a way which enables the state to impose its own ends on them. However, as the contradiction develops between the formal freedom of property law for the few and the "spiritual" freedom of all, the Christian religion emerges through its inheritance from the Romans of the universalized "infinite value" of the free person. But since there is little or no actual freedom for the newly Christianized masses of the Roman Empire, Christian subjectivity acquires a "soul" only by rejection of Rome's corrupt institutions. Because of this rejection, the early Christians downgrade all public ethical life, even family ties, in favor of the duties of discipleship. Hegel says that Jesus, because of his "passivity under the domination of an alien might which was despised," could "find freedom only in his heart, only in the void."[74] The precept to give to Caesar what is Caesar's and to God what is God's evades the question of what belongs to Caesar and what to God. As Rose points out, failure to answer this question leads to imperialism: with "the encroachment of Caesar on God, or God on Caesar... Each will be corrupted… and only capable of suppressing." In Hegel's view, the Reformation in Germany, in overthrowing the "terrible discipline of culture" in the Christian world, had made the "principle of free spirit" the "banner of the world." In Germany however, this had been merely a subjective development. The Revolution in France represented a more "objective spirit"; but the French had made a revolution without a Reformation.[75]

Hegel's *Philosophy of Religion* takes a swipe at the Enlightenment for its "indifference towards the content… [with] mere opinion [and] despair involved in its renunciation of the truth." Regarding the doctrines of the revealed religion, Hegel says that philosophy (his) "seems to be opposed to the church" because, while recognizing the historical necessity of the religious "form of representation," which is made universally accessible to the masses through the medium of the church, it refuses to be bound by the form. For in the "locale" of biblical and church history there is only the representation of the world of the past, which cannot and must not rule over the present. In the world of the present, true inwardization is a "spiritual now," which is both the negation of immediacy and the grasping of its consummation as a future. In the representation and particularization of life lived through the church, spiritual being is only implicit; it lacks the "absolute singularity of presence to self." Hegel's inwardizing can only take place through the "return from appearance" to the Concept, i.e., through the thinking reason of the free spirit, returning into the "inner place" of *the community and its organization.* Like Aristotle's "practical intelligence," the community imitates the higher realms; and for Hegel the community can only raise itself from the earth towards heaven because in the world it has "heaven within itself." Following the kingdom of "naïve religion" and the republic of the materialist Enlightenment comes "the third estate," the "community of philosophy." Hegel's view of the church is historical; and his critique of its theology is philosophical. The job of philosophical/logical "proof" is "to show that in point of fact there is a knowledge which advances neither by unmixed immediacy nor unmixed mediation."[76] This knowledge is Hegel's *Science of Logic* and the "intellectually comprehended" history that is philosophically actualized in his *Phenomenology of Spirit.*[77]

Raya Dunayevskaya sees Hegel as presenting ideas that "'think', not sequentially, but *con*sequentially, related to other Ideas that emerge out of historic ground, and do not care where all this might lead to, including transformation into opposite."[78] Hegel sees that the antinomies in Kantian thought (Freedom and Necessity, Custom and Law, etc.) are homologous to the dichotomy of the state and civil society, while at the same time they repeat the division in Roman Law between persons and things. Similarly, Marx, in the *Grundrisse*, shows how capital posits people as persons who have "rights" or/and as things, i.e., as labor-power. The theory of commodity fetishism developed in the first chapter of *Capital* is often seen as simply an exposition of how relations between persons become relations between things, mediated by the abstraction of money in the market. But, as Rose points out, the theory of fetishism also accounts for the illusions of "personification" which are intrinsic to the juridical categories of commodity, capital and money:

> The juridical opposition of free subjects and subjected things, which characterizes not only relations between different classes but also the relation of the individual to itself in modern states, forms the speculative core of Hegel's and of Marx's thinking.[79]

This speculative core is, however, done away with if, as has been the case with some of the theorists discussed in this book (such as Postone and Jappe), capital or "value" is identified with an allegedly Hegelian "totalizing subject" of congealed dead labor run amok in the sphere of circulation, free from the dialectic of living laborers and capital. On the Left generally there is a hostility or indifference towards philosophy which goes back a lot further than postmodernism and "post-Marxisms." It takes off from Engels' notorious claim, in *Ludwig Feuerbach and the End of Classical German Philosophy* (1888) about the dialectical legacy of "Marxism": "That which survives independently of all earlier philosophies is the science of thought and its laws—formal logic and dialectics. Everything else is subsumed in the positive science of nature and history." Even post-Marx Marxists, such as Cyril Smith, who reject Engels' version of "materialism," have invoked Marx's critique of Hegel for making the philosopher merely the "yardstick" of the alienated world.[80] A more nuanced interpretation of Marx's critique of the Hegelian dialectic is offered by Maurice Merleau-Ponty in a 1947 essay: if the philosopher "abandons the illusion of contemplating the totality of fulfilled history and feels himself, like other men, caught in it, and before a future to build, then philosophy realizes itself and vanishes as separate philosophy." This insight is made possible by Marx's conception of totality in relation to the "human factor" combined with the struggle against the fragmentation of the personality in the capitalist workplace. Marx, in taking up the "human object," was "carrying to its concrete consequences the Hegelian concept of 'spirit phenomenon.'"[81]

For Kant, the object world is constituted by an unknowable thing-in-itself, which is distinguished, firstly, from the transcendental synthesis of the pure forms of intuition—space and time—"given" to the knowing subject in the world of appearances, and secondly, from the pure categories of a priori understanding which are the condition of the possibilities of experience, i.e., of what can be thought. Lukács points out that the Hegelian perspective of totality is already implied by Kantian idealism, which contains the ideas of God and the Good in forms limited to regulative, not constitutive functions. This dualism of the rational and irrational which constitutes the dichotomy of the world—between the abstract morality of the bourgeois subject and the unknowable (and therefore impersonal) "god" or "freedom"— is at the heart of Fichte's statement about "the absolute projection of an object the origin of which no account can be given," resulting in the space between projection and the thing projected being "dark and void... the *projectio per hiatum irrationalem*."[82]

Whereas Kant takes the transcendental subject and its categories as given, Fichte transforms Kantian practical reason by conceiving the subject as the *creator*. Fichte attempts to overcome Kantian dualism by deriving the whole world of experience from the pure identity of the "absolute ego." As a foundational *act*, the ego, as the "I," posits itself in essential relation with the not-I. Once the not-I is understood as another free self, the resulting intersubjectivity constitutes a "free moral agent" resembling the Jacobin/Rousseauian general will as much as any deity. As in this process Fichte's absolute ego has absolute knowledge of its own postulates, the Kantian notion of the unknowable thing-in-itself is eliminated. As Rose comments, Fichte represents "an instrumental rationalism determined by the commodity form, and incapable of grasping the totality."[83]

Lukács sees Fichte's identity philosophy as presenting a truly bourgeois and capitalist subjectivity, because the antinomies in bourgeois thought represent the locking of *both* bourgeois and proletarian subjectivity into the "immediacy" of the reified relations of the commodity economy. Capital is not merely *external* to the worker's consciousness. From the bourgeois point of view, Lukács says, to go beyond this immediacy towards a historical perspective of *totality* would be "suicidal," for it would expose bourgeois rule as transitory. For the proletarian on the other hand, despite the reification process which "cripples and atrophies," it "remains true that his humanity and soul are not changed into commodities." If, in the commodity, the worker recognizes herself and her relations with capital as an object-object relation, then the actuality of the "split" between subjectivity and objectivity in his or her "total personality" can be *made conscious*. But the making of revolutionary consciousness implies that a mediation is needed to overcome the immediacy of reification, otherwise "the unmediated consciousness of the commodity" remains "precisely an awareness of abstract isolation" and of the "merely abstract relationship" to the material antagonism that creates it. As we have seen, Lukács' attempted solution to the problem of mediation involves the distinction he makes between the given "psychological" consciousness of the proletariat—of what is—and its "imputed" revolutionary consciousness—of what ought to be.[84] Although Lukács does criticize Engelsian Marxism for lapsing into a metaphysical materialism in which the reflecting consciousness of the subject is determined by the reflected object, there is a tendency in Lukács towards the opposite error: of positing a subject-object *identity*. This results in Lukács bringing in a *deus ex machine*—in effect an impersonal Fichtean subjectivity—in the form of the vanguard party.

The totality is itself riddled with contradictions and negativity if it fails to transcend the value form of production relations and their reflection in the "Subject," whether the Subject be the Party or, even the spontaneous revolt of the masses. Hegel's dialectic of "absolute negativity" signifies for Peter Hudis and Kevin Anderson, "not only the negation of external obstacles, but also the negation of the earlier negation. The power of negativity gets turned back on the self, upon the internal as well as external barriers to self-movement."[85] Since the eruption of economic crisis in 2008, there have been massive mobilizations in various parts of the world for social justice, some of which, as in the "Arab Spring" that began in 2011, have overthrown corrupt, repressive regimes and brought new possibilities for radical change. John Holloway warns in his book, *Change the World Without Taking Power*, against the error of either seeing economic crisis as an "opportunity" for revolution or as a "creative destruction" (Schumpeter's term) which might lead to further attempts at capitalist "restructuring" under a "new paradigm." Crisis, Holloway insists, is "essentially open"; to *define* it as restructuring between paradigms inevitably involves a "closure" of thought which rules out the rupture of capital and is blind to the world of struggle: "The moving force of crisis is the drive for freedom, the reciprocal flight of capital and anti-labor, the mutual repulsion of capital and humanity. The first moment of revolution is purely negative." What must further happen, Holloway contends, is the "considered rejection of capitalism as a mode of organization" and the "militant construction of alternatives to capitalism. They come later (or may do)." But if the "positive" in the struggle is the assertion of that which "exists in the mode of being denied," then how is the denial overcome? Holloway calls for "different" sorts of political actions, which "transform the experience of social life." Rather than a "continuous process of organization-building . . . there must an accumulation of practices of oppositional self-organization, but this should be thought of not as linear accumulation, but as a cumulative breaking of linearity. . . . Think of an anti-politics of *events* rather than a politics of organization."[86] Like several other theorists I have discussed in these pages, the originality of Holloway's "spontaneism" lies mainly in how he approaches the problem; in his case through engagement with Adorno's critical theory—which was itself an engagement with Lukács' theory of reification and commodity fetishism. Holloway does not however offer any praxis that gets beyond the debate of 1952–1953, involving Anton Pannekoek, Cornelius Castoriadis and C. L. R. James.

In the present political situation, Left-wing activism, directed against the greed of "fat cats," "banksters" and "predator" financiers, argues that these "greedy" elements, rather than the workers and retirees, should be made to "pay for the crisis." But can such "anti-capitalist politics" avoid falling in with some dubious popular-frontism for the purpose of turning the "People" against one fraction of the capitalist class deemed to be "unproductive," "predatory," or even "parasitical," and in support of a "progressive" fraction seen as "productive," "entrepreneurial" and "anti-monopolist"? To be sure, the revolutionary bourgeois thinkers of the eighteenth-century who waged ideological war on "Old Corruption" and *anciens régimes* did not think they were fighting for the right of a tiny minority to accumulate obscenely vast fortunes through the labor of others, who would be left with comparatively little (Plato, Aristotle and Aquinas likewise saw gross class inequalities as immoral, irrational and socially destructive). But the current focus—by liberal rationalists and Leftist critics of capitalist "decadence"—on the gap between present-day capitalist reality and Paineite and Smithian (or later social democratic) ideals misses the important point made by Gaspar Tamas: that capitalism cannot be defeated simply on the ideological or moral level; for Marx, as the poet of "Faustian demonism," effective critique of Capital could only be gained through "wading through the muck of estrangement."[87]

Today the capitalist crisis is so deep that the relative proportion of value going to capital as against labor must be increased for economic growth to restart and create another boom. Even taxing the rich "till the pips squeak"—as the Labour Party's Chancellor of the Exchequer Dennis Healy threatened to do during the British fiscal crisis of the 1970s—would not be enough to provide that spur. Peter Hudis argues:

> It is a staple of both vulgar bourgeois economists and vulgar 'Marxism' to conceive of social wealth as being reducible to the revenue paid out to workers on the one hand and to capitalists on the other—without recognizing that the bulk of the value produced in capitalism is 'consumed' neither by workers nor by capitalists but by capital itself. Economic development in capitalism primarily occurs through productive consumption—by capital itself (as against the capitalists) consuming an ever greater-share of the social wealth as it "becomes big with value." In a word, the greater quantities of value that capital needs to get the economy moving on an ever-expanding scale can ultimately come from one and only one source—from living labor.[88]

To pose the question of "what is wealth" must also consider the question, "what kind of work should people do?" For the classical political economists, being "productive" meant engaging in production of surplus value; "unproductive" meant frivolously living off the revenue rather than using it "productively." In the "Unpublished Chapter Six" of *Capital*, Marx employs, in contrast, the "power of abstraction" to show that, from the point of view of political economy, Milton, for example, must have been unproductive because he spent years writing *Paradise Lost* only to sell the manuscript for five pounds; whereas a hack who turns out political economy manuals at the direction of his publisher is productive. The hack's product "is from the outset subsumed under capital, and comes into being only for the purpose of increasing that capital." The "unproductiveness" of Milton on the other hand, clearly better represents for Marx "the absolute unfolding of man's creative abilities," because "Milton produced his *Paradise Lost* for the same reason that a silk-worm produces silk. It was an activity of his nature."[89]

Political economy tried to explain how society worked as expression of "human nature," but could not explain why social relations seemed to be determined by relations between commodities. For Marx, value is a "purely social" reality and capital is "value in process" ("valorization"). But value is not wealth. Against the Lassallean socialists who founded German Social Democracy, Marx insists in the *Critique of the Gotha Program* that "labor is *not* the source of all wealth"; because *nature* also is a source of wealth, though under the rule of capital wealth takes the form of capital. The possibility of creating a society based on real wealth rather than the value-form is certainly presupposed by the development of the productive forces and the self-development of the class engaged in production, but technological progress and "productiveness" in themselves do not produce real wealth; for under "human control" wealth would express the absolute unfolding of humans' creative abilities as an end-in-itself.

(2013)

NOTES

1. Alisdair MacIntyre, *Whose Justice? Which Rationality?* (University of Notre Dame Press: 1988), p. 1.
2. MacIntyre, p. 162–63.
3. Murray Bookchin, *The Ecology of Freedom* (Palo Alto: Cheshire Books, 1982), pp. 106-9 and pp. 221–22.
4. Jose Perez Adan, *Reformist Anarchism, 1800–1936: A Study of the Feasibility of Anarchism* (London: Merlin, 1992), pp. 184–86, pp. 216–23.
5. MacIntyre, pp. 316–20.
6. Quoted in Isaac Ilyich Rubin, *The History of Economic Thought* (London: Pluto Press, 1979), p. 70.
7. Rubin, *History of Economic Thought*, pp. 67–75.
8. Adan, pp. 184–86.
9. Marx, *Theories of Surplus Value, Vol. II* (London: Lawrence and Wishart, 1969), p. 166.
10. Marx, *Capital, Vol. I* (London: Penguin, 1976), pp. 493–94.
11. Marx, *Grundrisse* (London: Penguin, 1973), pp. 158–59.
12. Quoted in Andrew Kliman, *Marx's Concept of Intrinsic Value: On the Unity of Value, Fetishism and the Analysis of Capitalist Production in Capital* (Chicago: News and Letters Publications, 2003), p. 3
13. Marx, *Capital, Vol. I*, p. 128.
14. Marx, *Grundrisse*, p. 104.
15. Marx, *Capital, Vol. II* (London: Penguin 1978), p. 509.
16. Marx, *Grundrisse*, pp. 158–59.
17. Lukács, *History and Class Consciousness*, p. 159.
18. Lukács, *History and Class Consciousness*, p. 149.
19. Lukács, *History and Class Consciousness*, p. 51.
20. Lukács, *History and Class Consciousness*, p. 83.
21. Marx, *Capital, Vol. I*, p. 164.
22. Lukács, *History and Class Consciousness*, p. 13.
23. Dunayevskaya, *The Power of Negativity*, pp. 218–21.
24. Hegel, *Lectures on the History of Philosophy, Vol. III* (London: Kegan Paul, 1892), pp. 156–62.
25. Hegel, *Lectures, Vol. III*, pp. 156–62.
26. Lukács, *History and Class Consciousness*, p. 155.
27. Lukács, *History and Class Consciousness*, p. 164.
28. Rosa Luxemburg, *The Accumulation of Capital: An Anti-Critique,* (New York: Modern Reader, 1972), p. 77.
29. Dunayevskaya, *Rosa Luxemburg*, pp. 31–50.
30. Immanuel Kant, *Idea for a Universal History from a Cosmopolitan Point of View,* (New York: Bobbs-Merrill, 1986), pp. 249–62. www.marxists.org/reference/subject/ethics/kant/universal-history.htm
31. Gaspar Tamas, "Telling the Truth about Class," *Socialist Register* (2006).

32. Lukács, *History and Class Consciousness*, p. 208.
33. Tamas, "Telling the Truth about Class."
34. Tamas, "Telling the Truth about Class."
35. *Manifesto of the Communist Party of Germany*, trans. Helen Macfarlane, appendix to David Black, *Helen MacFarlane.*
36. P. Hudis, "Perspectives 2007," International Marxist-Humanist Organization Pamphlet (Chicago: 2008).
37. Francis Fukuyama, "The End of History," *National Interest,* No. 16, 1989.
38. Perry Anderson, *Zones of Engagement* (London: Verso, 1992), p. 366.
39. Anderson, *Zones,* pp. 315–16.
40. Friedrich Engels, "Ludwig Feuerbach and the End of German Classical Philosophy," *Marx and Engels Collected Works, Vol. 26* (New York: International Publishers, 1975); Kevin B. Anderson, *Lenin, Hegel and Western Marxism* (University of Illinois Press: 1995), pp. 12–15.
41. Perry Anderson, *Zones,* pp. 286–87.
42. Hegel, *Philosophy of Right* (Oxford: 1942), p. 123, quoted in Lukács, *Young Hegel*, p. 481.
43. Hegel, Phenomenology of Spirit, Baillie trans. (London: Allen & Unwin, 1931), p. 542, p. 546.
44. Alexandre Kojève, *Introduction to the Reading of Hegel* (Cornell University Press: 1980) pp. 162–63.
45. Hegel, *Phenomenology,* Baillie trans. p. 808.
46. Marx, "Excerpt Notes on Absolute Knowledge," appendix to Peter Hudis, *Marx's Concept of the Alternative to Capitalism* (Leiden-Boston: Brill, 2012), pp. 216–21.
47. Kojève, *Introduction to the Reading of Hegel,* p. 167.
48. Hegel, *Phenomenology,* Baillie trans., p. 808.
49. Lukács, *Young Hegel*, p. 538.
50. Lukács, *Young Hegel*, pp. 537–68.
51. Lukács, *Young Hegel*, p. 467.
52. Lukács, *Young Hegel*, p. 545–46.
53. Rose, *Hegel Contra Sociology*, p. 186.
54. Hegel, *Phenomenology,* Miller trans., p. 492.
55. Raya Dunayevskaya Collection. Wayne State University: microfilm no. 10923–41, 5/13/87.
56. Dunayevskaya Collection, microfilm no. 10923–41.
57. Marx, *Critique of the Gotha Program* (Moscow: Progress Publishers, 1970).
58. Hegel, *Phenomenology,* Baillie trans., p. 804; Dunayevskaya, *The Philosophic Moment of Marxist-Humanism* (Chicago: News and Letters Publications, 1989), p. 27, now included in *The Power of Negativity* (Lanham, MD: Lexington Books, 2002).
59. Hegel, *Philosophy of Mind,* p. 386.
60. Dunayevskaya, *Philosophic Moment*, p. 27.
61. C.L.R. James, *Notes on Dialectics* (London: Alison and Busby 1980), p. 219.
62. Leon Trotsky, *The Death Agony of Capitalism and the Tasks of the Fourth International: The Transitional Program,* Part 1 (New York: Pathfinder Press, 1983). www.marxists.org/archive/trotsky/1938/tp/tp-text.htm
63. James, Lee and Chaulieu, *Facing Reality*, p. 110.
64. Dunayevskaya,"Communism, Marxism, and Liberty—The American Humanist Tradition," Raya Dunayevskaya Collection, Wayne State University, microfilm no. 12514.
65. Dunayevskaya, "Not by Practice Alone, 1984–87" (May 19, 1987), in Raya Dunayevskaya Collection, microfilm no. 10955.
66. Castoriadis-Pannekoek correspondence. www.marxists.org/archive/pannekoe/1953/socialisme-ou-barbarisme.htm
67. Dunayevskaya Collection, 10901-3.
68. Castoriadis-Pannekoek correspondence, op. cit.
69. Marx, *Grundrisse*, p. 107.
70. Dunayevskaya, *Power of Negativity*, pp. 337–40.

71. Gillian Rose, *Mourning Becomes the Law* (Cambridge: 1996), pp. 2–5.

72. Jean-François Lyotard, *The Postmodern Condition: A Report on Knowledge* (University of Minnesota Press: 1979).

73. Rose, *Mourning Becomes the Law,* pp. 2–5.

74. Quoted by Rose, in *Hegel Contra Sociology,* p. 123 (Rose's translation from *Der Geist in Christentums, Schriften 1796–1800*, 500, tr. 285).

75. Rose, *Hegel Contra Sociology,* pp. 116–18.

76. Hegel, "Christianity as the Consummate Religion," *Philosophy of Religion, Vol. III*, published in *GWF Hegel: Theologian of the Spirit,* edited by P. Hodgson (Nashville: Fortress Press, 1993).

77. Hegel, *Phenomenology*, Baillie trans., p. 808.

78. Dunayevskaya, *Power of Negativity*, p. 133.

79. Gillian Rose, *The Dialectic of Nihilism* (London: Blackwell, 1984), p. 3.

80. Cyril Smith, "Critical Comments on Raya Dunayevskaya's Notes on the Smaller Logic," *The Hobgoblin,* No. 5. 2003. www.thehobgoblin.co.uk/journal/H5cyrilsmithonrd.html

81. Maurice Merleau-Ponty, "Marxism and Philosophy," *Sense and None-sense*, translated by Hubert and Patricia Dreyfus (Northwestern University Press: 1992), pp. 125–36. Quoted in Dunayevskaya, *Power of Negativity*, p. 111.

82. Lukács, *History and Class Consciousness*, pp. 291–97.

83. Rose, *Hegel Contra Sociology*, p. 32.

84. Lukács, *History and Class Consciousness,* pp.168–72.

85. Peter Hudis and Kevin B. Anderson's introduction to Dunayevskaya, *Power of Negativity,* p. xviii.

86. John Holloway, *Change the World Without Taking Power: The Meaning of Revolution Today* (London: Pluto Press, 2002), pp. 204–15.

87. Tamas, "Telling the Truth about Class."

88. Peter Hudis, "Why a New International Marxist-Humanist Organization? Why Now? The Economic, Political, and Philosophical Context," www.usmarxisthumanists.org/articles/

89. Marx, *Capital, Vol. I*, p. 1044.

Bibliography

BOOKS

Adan, Jose Perez. *Reformist Anarchism 1800–1936: A Study of the Feasibility of Anarchism.* London: Merlin, 1992.
Adorno, Theodor. *Minima Moralia.* London: New Left Books, 1974.
Anderson, Kevin B. *Lenin, Hegel and Western Marxism.* University of Illinois Press: 1995.
—*Marx at the Margins: On Nationalism, Ethnicity and Non-Western Societies.* University of Chicago Press: 2010.
Anderson, Perry. *Zones of Engagement.* London: Verso, 1992.
Apostolidès, Jean-Marie; Dunné, Boris. *Ivan Chtcheglov.* Paris: Editions Allia, 2006.
Aristotle. *Nicomachean Ethics.* Indianapolis: Hacket Publishing, 1999.
—*Politics.* Indianapolis: Hacket Publishing, 1998.
Balakian, Anna. *Surrealism: The Road to the Absolute.* Chicago University Press: 1987.
Benjamin, Walter. *Charles Baudelaire.* London: Verso, 1976.
—*Illuminations.* London: Fontana, 1970.
—*The Arcades Project.* Ed. and trans. H. Eiland and K. McLaughlin. Harvard University Press: 1999.
Berman, Marshall. *All That Is Solid Melts into Air.* London: Verso, 1982.
Black, David. *Helen MacFarlane: A Feminist, Revolutionary Journalist and Philosopher in Mid-Nineteenth Century England.* Lanham, MD: Lexington Books, 2004.
Bookchin, Murray. *The Ecology of Freedom.* Palo Alto: Cheshire Books, 1982.
Bracken, Len. *Guy Debord—Revolutionary.* Venice Cal: Feral House, 1997.
Breton, André. *What Is Surrealism? Selected Writings.* Ed. Franklin Rosemont. London: Pluto, 1978.
Campbell, Joseph (ed.). *The Meaning of the Eleusinian Mysteries (Papers From the Eranos Yearbooks).* Princeton University Press: 1979.
Chtcheglov, Ivan. *Écrits Retrouvé.* Paris: Éditions Allia, 2006.
Cornford, Francis MacDonald. *From Religion to Philosophy.* Princeton Paperbacks: 1991.
—*Principium Sapientiae: A Study of the Origins of Greek Philosophical Thought.* Cambridge University Press: 1952.
—*The Unwritten Philosophy.* Cambridge University Press: 1940.
C. L. R. James, His Intellectual Legacies. Eds. S. R. Cudjoe and W. E. Cain. Massachusetts University Press: 1995.
Debord, Guy. *Society of the Spectacle.* Detroit: Black and Red, 1983.
—*Comments on the Society of the Spectacle.* Trans. Malcolm Imrie. London: Verso, 1998.

—(With Gianfranco Sanguinetti). *The Veritable Split in the International.* Trans. Lucy Forsyth, Michel Prigent. London: BM Chronos, 1985.
—*Complete Cinematic Works*. San Francisco: Bureau of Public Secrets, 2003. www.bopsecrets.org/SI/debord.films/— *Situationist International Anthology*, ed. Ken Knabb. Berkeley: Bureau of Public Secrets, 1989.
—*Guy Debord and the Situationist International: Texts and Documents*, ed. Tom McDonough (Cambridge: October Books, 2002).
Dunayevskaya, Raya. *Marxism and Freedom: From 1776 Until Today.* New York: Bookman Associates, 1957.
—*Philosophy and Revolution*, Lanham. MD: Lexington Books, 2003.
—*Rosa Luxemburg, Womens Liberation and Marx's Philosophy of Revolution.* University of Illinois Press: 1991.
—*The Marxist-Humanist Theory of State-Capitalism.* Chicago: News and Letters Publications, 1992.
—*The Power of Negativity.* Lanham, MD: Lexington Books, 2002.
—"Marx's Humanism Today," in *Socialist Humanism.* Ed. Erich Fromm. New York: Doubleday, 1965.
— *Marx's Capital and Today's Global Crisis.* Detroit: News and Letters Publications, 1978.
Engels, Friedrich. *Anti-Dühring.* Moscow: Progress Publishers, 1978.
— *Lugwig Feuerbach and the End of German Classical Philosophy.* University Press of the Pacific: 2005.
Fanon, Franz. *The Wretched of the Earth.* New York: Grove, 1965.
Farrington, Benjamin. *Science and Politics in the Ancient World.* London: Allen and Unwin, 1965.
Ferrarin, Alfredo. *Hegel and Aristotle.* Cambridge University Press: 2001.
Gershman, Herbert. *The Surrealist Revolution in France.* Ann Arbor Paperbacks: 1974.
Gombin, Richard. *The Origins of Modern Leftism.* London: Penguin, 1975.
Goode, Patrick. *Karl Korsch: A Study in Western Marxism*. London: Macmillan, 1979.
Hegel, George Wilhelm Friedrich. *The Difference between Fichte's and Schelling's System of Philosophy.* SUNY Press: 1977.
— *G. W. F. Hegel: Theologian of the Spirit (selected works on religion).* Ed. P. Hodgson. Nashville University Press: 1993.
—*Lectures on the History of Philosophy, Vol I.* London: Kegan Paul, 1892.
—*Lectures on the History of Philosophy, Vol. III.* London: Kegan Paul, 1892.
—*Phenomenology of Spirit.* Trans. J. B. Baillie. London: Allen & Unwin, 1931. *Phenomenology of Spirit.* Trans. A. V. Miller. Oxford University Press: 1977.
—*Science of Logic*. Trans. W. H. Johnston and L. G. Struthers. London: Allen & Unwin, 1951.
—*Selections from Hegel's Lectures on Aesthetics.* Trans. Bernard Bosanquet and W.M. Bryant, *The Journal of Speculative Philosophy* (London:1886). www.marxists.org/reference/archive/hegel/index.htm
—*System of Ethical Life* and *The First Philosophy of Spirit.* State University of New York Press: 2004.
—*Philosophy of Mind. Part 3 of Hegel's Encyclopedia of the Philosophical Sciences, Vol. III.* Oxford University Press: 1971.
—*Philosophy of Right.* Oxford University Press: 1942.
Heidegger, Martin. *Basic Writings.* London: Routledge, 1978.
Hirsch, Arthur. *The French Left.* Montreal: Black Rose, 1982.
Holloway, John. *Change the World Without Taking Power: the Meaning of Revolution Today.* London: Pluto Press, 2002.
Hudis, Peter. *Harry McShane and the Scottish Roots of Marxist-Humanism.* Glasgow: John Maclean Society Pamphlets, 1992.
—*Marx's Concept of the Alternative to Capitalism*. Leiden-Boston: Brill, 2012.
Hume, David. *An Inquiry Concerning Human Understanding.* London: Pearson, 1995.
Internationale Situationiste 1958–1969. Paris: Éditions Champ Libre, 1975.
James, C.L.R. *The Future in the Present.* London: Alison and Busby, 1980.
—*Notes on Dialectics.* London: Alison and Busby 1980.

—(with Grace C. Lee and Pierre Chaulieu) *Facing Reality: The New Society, Where to Look for It, How to Bring It Closer* (Detroit: Bewick, 1974.
Jappe, Anselm. *Guy Debord.* University of California Press: 1999.
Kahn, Charles H. (editor). *The Art and Thought of Heraclitus: An Edition of the Fragments with Translation and Commentary.* Cambridge University Press: 1981.
Kant, Immanuel. *Idea for a Universal History from a Cosmopolitan Point of View.* New York: Bobbs-Merrill, 1986.
Kaufman, Vincent. *Guy Debord: Revolution in the Service of Poetry* University of Minnesota Press: 2006.
Kliman, Andrew. *Marx's Concept of Intrinsic Value—On the Unity of Value, Fetishism and the Analysis of Capitalist Production in* Capital. Chicago: News and Letters, 2003.
—*Reclaiming Marx's* Capital—*A Refutation of the Myth of Inconsistency.* Lanham, MD: Lexington Books, 2008.
Kojève, Alexander. *Introduction to the Reading of Hegel.* Cornell University Press: 1980.
Korsch, Karl. *Marxism and Philosophy* New York: Monthly Review Press, 1970.
Lefebvre, Henri. *Critique of Everyday Life, Vol. I* Trans. J. Moore, G. Elliott. London: Verso, 2008.
Lenin, Vladmir Illich. *Collected Works Vol. 38.* Moscow: Progress Publishers, 1965.
Lukács, Georg. *History and Class Consciousness.* London: Merlin, 1971.
—*The Young Hegel.* London: Merlin Press, 1977.
Luxemburg, Rosa. *The Rosa Luxemburg Reader,* eds. Peter Hudis and Kevin B. Anderson. New York: Monthly Review Press, 2004.
—*The Accumulation of Capital: An Anti-Critique*. New York: Modern Reader, 1972.
Lyotard, François. *The Postmodern Condition: A Report on Knowledge.* University of Minnesota Press: 1979.
MacIntyre, Alisdair. *Whose Justice? Which Rationality?* University of Notre Dame Press: 1988.
Marcus, Greil. *Lipstick Traces: A Secret History of the Twentieth Century.* Harvard University Press: 1990.
Marcuse, Herbert. *Hegel's Ontology and the Theory of Historicity* (translation and introduction by Seyla Benhabib). MIT Press: 1989.
—*Reason and Revolution*. London: Routledge, 1973.
Marx, Karl. *Capital Vol. I.* London: Penguin, 1976.
—*Capital, Vol. II.* London: Penguin, 1978.
—*Capital, Vol. III.* London: Penguin, 1978.
—*Critique of the Gotha Program.* Moscow: Progress Publishers, 1970.
—*Early Writings.* London: Penguin, 1973.
—*Grundrisse.* London: Penguin, 1973.
—*Theories of Surplus Value, Vol. II.* London: Lawrence and Wishart, 1969.
—*Value: Studies by Marx.* London: New Park Publications, 1976.
—*Marx and Engels Collected Works, Vol.22*. New York: International Publishers, 1989.
—*Karl Marx Texts and Method.* Ed. T. Carver. Oxford University Press: 1975.
McShane, Harry (and Joan Smith). *Harry McShane: No Mean Fighter.* London: Pluto Press, 1978.
Mension, Jean-Michel. *The Tribe.* London: Verso, 2002.
Merleau-Ponty, Maurice, *Sense and None-sense.* Trans. Hubert & Patricia Dreyfus. Northwestern University Press: 1992.
Milton, Nan. *John MacLean.* London: Pluto Press, 1973.
Müller-Doohm, Stefan. *Adorno: A biography.* London: Polity, 2005.
Pannekoek, Anton; and Korsch, Karl. *Lenin and Philosophy.* London: Merlin, 1975.
Plato. *The Republic.* Trans. F. M. Cornford. Oxford University Press: 1945.
—*Parmenides*. Trans. A. K. Whitaker. Newburyport, MA: Focus Publishing, 1996.
Postone, Moishe. *Time, Labor and Social Domination.* Cambridge University Press: 1996.
Rose, Gillian. *The Broken Middle: Out of Our Ancient Society.* Oxford: Blackwell, 1995.
—*The Dialectic of Nihilism.* London: Blackwell, 1984.
—*Hegel Contra Sociology.* London: Continuum, 2000.

—*Mourning Becomes the Law*. Cambridge University Press: 1996.
Rubin, Isaac Ilyich, *The History of Economic Thought*. London: Pluto Press, 1979.
Seaford, Richard. *Money and the Early Greek Mind: Homer, Philosophy, Tragedy*. Cambridge University Press: 2004.
Smith, Cyril. *Marx at the Millenium*. London: Pluto Press, 1996.
Stirk, Peter. *Max Horkheimer: A New Interpretation*. Lanham, MD: Lexington Books, 1992.
Sohn-Rethel, Alfred. *Intellectual and Manual Labour: A Critique of Epistemology*. London: Macmillan, 1976.
Ste. Croix, Geoffrey. *Class Struggle in the Ancient Greek World*. Cornell University Press: 1998.
Thomson, George. *Aeschylus and Athens*. London: Lawrence and Wishart, 1941.
—*The First Philosophers: Studies in Ancient Greek Society*. London: Lawrence and Wishart, 1955.
Trotsky, Leon. *The Death Agony of Capitalism and the Tasks of the Fourth International*. New York: Pathfinder Press, 1983.

ARTICLES

Arthur, C. J. "Review of H. Williams' Hegel, Heraclitus and Marx's Dialectic; G. Reuten and M. Williams' *Value-Form and the State*; and T. Smith's *The Logic of Marx's Capital." Hegel Society of Great Britain Bulletin,* No. 23/24, 1991.
Burbidge, John W. "Hegel's Hat Trick," *Bulletin of the Hegel Society of Great Britain,* No. 39/40, 1999.
Calvert, Brian. "Slavery in Plato's Republic," *The Classical Quarterly, New Series, Vol. 37*, No. 2, 1987.
Castoriadis, Cornelius, "On the History of the Workers Movement," *Telos*, No. 30, 1976.
Chaulieu, Pierre (Cornelius Castoriadis) "Réponse au camarade Pannekoek," *Socialisme ou Barbarie* (April–June 1954).
Chaulieu, Pierre (Cornelius Castoriadis). "Sur le contenu du socialisme," *Socialisme ou Barbarie,* No. 22, July–September 1957.
Gaiger, Jason. "Art as Made and Sensuous: Hegel, Danto and the 'End of Art'." *Bulletin of the Hegel Society of Great Britain,* No. 41, 2000.
Hudis, Peter. "The Death of the Death of the Subject." *Historical Materialism*, 12:3, 2004.
Jappe, Anselm. "Who Is to Blame" (2011). www/libcom.org/library/who-blame-anselm-jappe
Jorn, Asger. "Détourned Painting." Exhibition Catalogue, Rive Gauche Gallery (May 1959). Trans. Thomas Y. Levin. www.cddc.vt.edu/sionline/si/painting.html
Kliman, Andrew. "A New Look at the Russian Revision of Marx's Concept of 'Directly Social Labor'." *News and Letters,* November–December 2005.
Korsch, Karl. "Marxism and Philosophy, and Ten Theses on Marxism." *Telos,* No. 26, 1975/76.
Lefort, Claude. "Interview." *Telos,* No. 30, 1976.
McShane, Harry. "Review of Raya Dunayevska's *Philosophy and Revolution." The Scottish Marxist-Humanist*, 1974. Reprinted in *Hobgoblin,* No. 5, 2003.
Nieuwenhuys, Constant. "Manifesto," *Reflex*, Amsterdam: 1948. www.cddc.vt.edu/sionline/presitu/manifesto.html
Sohn-Rethel, Alfred. "The Historical Materialist Theory of Knowledge" (in four parts). *Marxism Today* (March, April, May and June 1965).
Rockwell, Russell. "Hegel and Critical Social Theory: New Perspectives from the Marcuse Archives." *The Sociological Quarterly*, 45:1, 2004.
Pannekoek, Anton. "Discussion sur le probleme du parti révolutionnaire," *Socialisme ou Barbarie*, July–August 1952.
Rubin, Isaak I. "Abstract Labour and Value in Marx's System." *Capital and Class,* No. 5, 1978.
Rumney, Ralph. Interview. *Vague,* No. 22, 1989.

Smith, Cyril. "Critical Comments on Raya Dunayevskaya's Notes on the Smaller Logic." *The Hobgoblin,* No. 5. www.thehobgoblin.co.uk/journal/H5cyrilsmithonrd.html
Tamas, Gaspar. "Telling the Truth about Class." *Socialist Register, Vol. 42*, 2006.
Van der Linden, Marcel. "Socialisme ou Barbarie." *Left History,* 5:1, 1997.
Wandschneider, Dieter. "Nature and Dialectic of Nature in Hegel's Objective Idealism." *Bulletin of the Hegel Society of Great Britain*, No. 39/40, 1999.

Index

About the Author

David Black is an independent scholar and journalist living in London. His previous books are *1839: The Chartist Insurrection* (with Chris Ford, published 2012); *Helen Macfarlane: A Feminist, Revolutionary Journalist and Philosopher in Mid-19th Century England* (2004); and *Acid: A New Secret History of LSD* (2001).

www.ingramcontent.com/pod-product-compliance
Ingram Content Group UK Ltd.
Pitfield, Milton Keynes, MK11 3LW, UK
UKHW041122071026
15587UKWH00009B/91

9 780739 173954